Why was England the only country in Europe to maintain an all-male public theatre in the Renaissance? Stephen Orgel uses this question as the starting point of a fresh and stimulating exploration of the representation of gender in Elizabethan drama and society. Why were boys used to play female roles in drama, and how did such cross-dressing affect the plays of Shakespeare and his contemporaries? What was the place of women in the Renaissance theatre, either on stage or in the audience? And what did society make of those women who significantly and successfully violated accepted gender boundaries? At once provocative and witty, lucid and stylish, *Impersonations* will reshape our understanding of the Renaissance theatre, and make us rethink our own inadequate categories of gender, power and sexuality.

Impersonations

Impersonations

The performance of gender in
Shakespeare's England

Stephen Orgel
Stanford University

CAMBRIDGE
UNIVERSITY PRESS

Published by the Press Syndicate of the University of Cambridge
The Pitt Building, Trumpington, Cambridge CB2 1RP
40 West 20th Street, New York, NY 10011–4211, USA
10 Stamford Road, Oakleigh, Melbourne 3166, Australia

First published 1996

Printed in Great Britain at the University Press, Cambridge

A catalogue for this book is available from the British Library

Library of Congress cataloguing in publication data

Orgel, Stephen.
Impersonations: the performance of gender in Shakespeare's
England / Stephen Orgel.
p.   cm.
Includes bibliographical references and index.
ISBN 0 521 56065 X (hardback). – ISBN 0 521 56842 0 (paperback)
1. Shakespeare, William, 1564–1616 – Stage history – To 1625.
2. English drama – Early modern, 1500–1700 – History and criticism.
3. Shakespeare, William, 1564–1616 – Dramatic production.
4. Shakespeare, William, 1564–1616 – Characters – Women.   5. Theater –
England – Casting – History – 16th century.   6. Theater – England –
Casting – History – 17th century.   7. Child actors – England – History.
8. Gender identity in literature.   11. Women in literature.   I. Title.
PR3095.O74   1996
792'.0942031 – dc20   95-41287   CIP

ISBN 0521 56056X hardback
ISBN 0521 568420 paperback

Transferred to digital reprinting 2000
Printed in the United States of America

SE

In memory of

DUNCAN ASWELL

TOM STEHLING

ARTURO ISLAS

JACK WINKLER

GARY SPEAR

o beate Sesti,
vitae summa brevis spem nos vetat inchoare longam ...

Oh goodlooking fortunate Sestius, don't put your hope
    in the future;
   The night is falling; the shades are gathering around;
The walls of Pluto's shadowy house are closing you in;
   There who will be lord of the feast? What will it matter,
What will it matter, there, whether you fell in love
    With Lycidas, this or that girl with him, or he with her?

Horace *Odes* 1.4, tr. David Ferry

The word Person . . . in latine signifies the *disguise,* or *outward appearance* of a man, counterfeited on the Stage; and sometimes more particularly that part of it, which disguiseith the face, as a Mask or Vizard: And from the Stage, hath been translated to any Representer of speech and action, as well in Tribunalls, as Theaters. So that a *Person,* is the same that an *Actor* is, both on the Stage and in common conversation; and to *Personate,* is to Act, or *Represent* himselfe, or an other.

Hobbes, *Leviathan* I.16

Contents

✼

Illustrations

Preface

This book began, for me, long before gender construction was a fashionable topic and postmodernism the dominant discourse. For two of my four years at the Horace Mann School for Boys in New York in the late 1940s, transvestite theatre was an unproblematic reality. Like several other members of the Drama Club, I regularly played both male and female roles, with no sense that any stigma was attached to performing as a woman. This is how the Drama Club had always operated; but in my junior year, in 1948, the policy suddenly changed: for *Our Town* and *The Man Who Came to Dinner* we brought in actresses from a nearby girls' school, and thereafter transvestite theatre was a thing of the past. What strikes me now as odd is how seamless the transition was. Not only was it never discussed publicly, but more interestingly, nobody ever asked why the change had been made – it did not occur to me to wonder why in my sophomore year I was playing women without awkwardness or comment, and a year later to do so had become unthinkable. It took almost forty years for me to realize that I had lived through a paradigm shift without noticing it.

Once I did notice it, however, I became intensely curious. The drama coach, Fred Little, a charismatic and inventive director and an extraordinarily sympathetic teacher, was in his eighties, living in retirement in Vermont. I had admired him immensely, and consider him one of the formative influences of my school years. I had last exchanged letters with him at least thirty years before, but I phoned him out of the blue and posed my question: how did it happen? Had parents complained? Had boys started to refuse to dress as women? Not at all, he assured me; nothing had happened: "I just didn't think it was a good idea." But why not? His first answer was clearly an evasion: the boys simply couldn't do it convincingly. When I pointed out that we did not make very convincing men either, he wholeheartedly agreed, and – cautiously – went on to the explanation I had, I suppose, been waiting to hear: "It was turning the boys into pansies."

So there it was – the very explanation that William Prynne or John Rainoldes would have given me three hundred and fifty years before. But Fred Little was no descendant of Renaissance antitheatrical polemicists; what he, and I, had participated in was a genuine change in sexual morality. Five years earlier what the school would have considered dangerous to the morals of American adolescent boys was precisely the presence of women at close quarters, and travesty was the prophylactic against erotic contamination; suddenly, in 1948, travesty itself was the danger, and women had to be imported to save us from becoming pansies. Everything we were taught in biology and sex education classes to the contrary notwithstanding, gender was obviously not a fixed category, neither in 1948 nor in 1600. I decided not to reveal to my old teacher that his fears had been realized in me, but from the moment of that phone conversation, writing this book became irresistible.

I owe a great debt to many friends and colleagues. Anne Barton, Catherine Belsey, A. R. Braunmuller, Alan Bray, Jonathan Crewe, Simon During, Marjorie Garber, Linda Gregerson, Jonathan Goldberg, Stephen Greenblatt, David Halperin, Barbara Johnson, Ann Rosalind Jones, Coppélia Kahn, Adrian Kiernander, Joan Linton, David Lee Miller, Steven Mullaney, Karen Newman, Alan Sinfield and Nicola Watson read (or heard) and commented on sections of the manuscript; Heather Dubrow in addition supplied me with a number of invaluable bibliographical references. For citations, elucidations and examples, I am grateful to Anne Beckwith Blake, Steve Danzis, Margreta de Grazia, Ursula Heise, Christopher Highley, William Kerrigan, Laura Levine, Patricia Parker, David Riggs, David Harris Sacks, Winfried Schleiner, Paul Seaver, Michael Shapiro, Bruce Smith, John Tinker, Sophie Tomlinson, Robert K. Turner, Mary Wack and Michael Wyatt. Marion Trousdale has been an unfailing source of information and wisdom; Leonard Barkan, Terry Castle and Randall Nakayama were the best of listeners and the most judicious of critics. I also gratefully acknowledge the support of Stanford University, which was generous and unfailing, and of the National Endowment for the Humanities, which awarded me a senior fellowship. Three sections of this book have appeared in print: a much earlier (and really rudimentary) version of chapter 2 with a rather different argument, appeared under the title "Nobody's Perfect, or Why Did the English Stage Take Boys for Women?" in *South Atlantic Quarterly* 88:1 (Winter 1989); a version of chapter 5 appeared under the title "Insolent Women and Manlike Apparel" in *Textual Practice* 9:1 (Spring 1995); and some of chapter 7 appeared under the title "The Subtexts of *The Roaring Girl*" in Susan Zimmerman, ed., *Erotic Politics*, (New York and London, 1992). For the final text, Peter Holland was an acute, learned and helpful critic. Most of all, I am indebted to Peter Stallybrass, who not only encouraged me to talk out long sections of the book with him, but gave the manuscript the most detailed and generous of readings, and most of whose suggestions I have silently adopted.

Finally, I am grateful to David Ferry for allowing me to print a passage from his beautiful translation of Horace, *Odes* 1.4 in the dedication.

꙼

I

Introduction

This book began as an investigation of a specialized and specific
issue. Its working title was *Why Did the English Stage Take Boys for
Women?* – a graceless title, no doubt, but one that articulates a question that seems to me a basic and irresistible one about the Elizabethan
theatre. It has not seemed so to three centuries of theatre historians,
who have treated it as a minor point, of interest primarily for its effect
on disguise plots. The matter has generally been disposed of by observing that the English were used to an all-male stage from generations of
university productions and mystery plays, the latter performed by the
all-male craft guilds, and that the appearance of women on stage was
forbidden because it was felt in the Renaissance to compromise their
modesty. This is probably correct as far as it goes, though as we shall
see, certain significant problems have been occluded in the case of the
craft guilds; but a glance across the channel reveals its inadequacy as an
explanation. French, Spanish and Italian society was just as familiar
with academic and guild performances, and quite as deeply concerned
with female virtue as England was, and none banned actresses from the
public stage. Actresses were, to be sure, a relatively new phenomenon
in continental theatres, first appearing around the middle of the sixteenth century; but by Shakespeare's time they were a commonplace
feature of the European stage – societies that maintained a public stage
expected to see women on it. The English equation of actresses with
whores was also common in France and Italy, but this was not seen as
an impediment to their performing in plays. Spain provides an even
more striking parallel. Spanish morality was far more restrictive of

women's behavior than English morality was; nevertheless, actresses appeared on Spanish stages with the explicit approval of both civil and ecclesiastical authorities – as did, moreover, transvestite boys. The problem of female chastity was sufficiently resolved, officially at least, in French and Spanish theatres merely by requiring that the actresses be married.[1]

There were, to be sure, countries besides England that proscribed women from the public stage – for example the Netherlands, and certain areas of Protestant Germany. But here it was theatre itself that was felt to be morally dangerous, and the acting profession therefore imperiled the virtue of men as well as women. In these societies, the solution was to dispense with the public stage entirely – actors were no more tolerable than actresses. Viewed in a European context, the English situation is anomalous.

Once we allow ourselves to address such issues, it is natural to look for explanations for them – explanations that will be both culturally specific and sufficiently broad to account for what appears, at least in the history of Renaissance theatre as we have constructed it, an uninflected and remarkably long-lived phenomenon. But to set the matter up as a question – why did the English stage take boys for women? – is in a sense to misrepresent it. The question conceals (and may, indeed, be a way of concealing) important prior and more basic issues. What is the relation between the construction of gender on the stage – any stage – and in society at large; why has the uniqueness of gender construction on the English stage never seemed problematic until now; and – perhaps even more substantive – what would qualify for us as an adequate explanation?

Indeed, to set the matter up as a question at all presupposes that there is an answer; but to answer a question so narrowly conceived is to close it off, and thereby to trivialize it. There are many possible kinds of answers, but they all lead to more questions; and ultimately it is the openness of the question, and the ambiguities and ambivalences of the two cultural situations – Renaissance and contemporary – generating it, that we must address. I am, then, not undertaking to answer a question but to raise one; to address an exfoliating cultural issue of which we can give many kinds of accounts, but none sufficient to settle the matter, for the matter is a process that is still going on. The question, at its deepest level, is how gender was constructed by Early Modern cultures; to ask this is also to ask how it is constructed by our own, and – more disturbingly – why it is constructed in that way. Whatever answers we give, the question will remain.

We might begin by observing that in its own time the issue did not seem like a question. It was the continental theatre that was, for English viewers, problematic and eccentric. "Our players are not as the players beyond the sea," wrote Thomas Nashe in *Pierce Penniless*, "a sort of squirting bawdy comedians, that have whores and common courtesans to play women's parts, and forbear no immodest speech or unchaste action that may provoke laughter."[2] The matter is presented as a self-evident index to the viciousness of foreigners. There were many polemical debates in England about the dangers to public morality of transvestite boy actors; but none that argued in favor of the introduction of women as an alternative. That part of the issue was not in question.

Nevertheless, the totalizing aspects of claims such as Nashe's need scrutiny: is it true that women never appeared on English stages? The claim, to begin with, can relate only to the public theatre; women commonly appeared as dancers in court masques throughout the Elizabethan and Jacobean periods, and under the patronage of Henrietta Maria, Charles I's French queen, they took speaking roles in court plays as well. The practice was not limited to the Frenchified world of Whitehall: the sizable role of the Lady in *Comus* was performed by the fifteen-year-old Lady Alice Egerton when Milton's masque was presented before her father, the Earl of Bridgewater, in 1634. But the point is not merely that remarks such as Nashe's refer only to the public stage; it is that the performer's amateur status made the whole difference: for those to whom theatre was not in itself problematical, there was no stigma whatever attached to women performing in plays, so long as they did not do it as a profession.

The problem then seems to be not with the effect of women on audiences, but specifically with women who define themselves as actresses and with audiences that are "public," that is, indiscriminately composed. But let us press further: how accurate is Nashe's claim even with regard to the public stage? It seems to imply not only a distinction between the theatres of England and the Continent, but a distinction that was categorical and permanent. Theatrical history has certainly read the English situation in this way. A recent attempt to understand the theatrical use of transvestite boys by invoking the concept of androgyny observes that English companies were all male, and had always been so: "the audience had never experienced anything else."[3] The unwillingness to interrogate the most basic information is characteristic of theatre history as a whole. It is certainly true that the professional theatre companies of Shakespeare's time included no women. But how do we know that the English public stage had always been exclusively male?

We do not know it. In fact, there is counterevidence bearing on the matter to be found even in the standard histories. Glynne Wickham cites the records of the London Lord Mayor's Shows in which payments to several women who took roles in the entertainments of 1523 and 1534 are recorded[4] – there were in London in the early sixteenth century professional women performers who were hired to appear in public entertainments. Wickham goes on to deduce what should be an important inference from these data: that "in the Middle Ages and in Tudor times, women could and did perform both as amateurs and professionals in so far as society would allow them to." The final cautious qualification is understandable, given the history of the discipline; Wickham does nothing further with his information, and the process of rethinking the gender assumptions of English theatre history on the basis of such evidence, or even of attempting to account for what appear, in English stage history as we understand it, striking anomalies, can barely be said to have begun.

That it *has* begun, however, is undeniable. Wickham in fact offered more evidence than this for the participation of women in medieval drama. In the late fifteenth century in Chester, a play of the Assumption of the Virgin is recorded as having been performed by "the wives of this town." In 1972 Rosemary Woolf challenged the evidence, arguing that the crucial word must be not "wives" but "weavers"; but then, having rejected the claim, she goes on to make an important observation: there is no reason to believe that women did not, in fact, "occasionally" perform in medieval drama.[5] That is, a medievalist writing in 1972 could find no reason to believe what historians of the theatre have simply taken for granted.[6] Woolf's paleographic argument, however, has in turn been undermined by more recent work: the REED volume on the Chester documents leaves no doubt that "wives" is in fact the correct reading in the surviving sources.[7] Indeed, as early as 1954 Jean Robertson and D. J. Gordon had found in the dramatic records of the London livery companies evidence that "women in Tudor pageants were by no means always impersonated by boys: in 1519 two maidens were engaged to play Our Lady and St. Elizabeth; and in 1534 four ladies played the Virgin Mary and her three attendants."[8]

So until the 1530s, at least, women seem to have performed unproblematically in guild and civic theatrical productions. The evidence for actresses on the English stage is not, however, limited to pre-Elizabethan times. I myself found two women apparently routinely performing professionally as theatrical singers in 1632. One was French, a Madame Coniack, and can perhaps be explained away as a foreign exception, but the other was named Mistress Shepard. I noted their existence in *Inigo Jones*,[9] but all my attempts to pursue the matter further drew blanks. These performers can hardly have been unique and have caused no contemporary comment; but are they basically anomalies or the tip of an iceberg? To my knowledge, though they appear in an easily available source, the printed text of Aurelian Townshend's *Tempe Restored*, only one other critic has expressed any interest in them – in the history of English theatre, they do not exist.

The exceptional critic, however, is worth attending to. Suzanne Gossett, in the course of a survey of women in Jacobean and Caroline masques, points out that the appearance of Madame Coniack in *Tempe Restored* deserves to be considered a genuinely symbolic moment in the history of the English stage. Coniack took the role of Circe; when confronted in the masque by Pallas Athena, played by a male actor, she banished the goddess with words that must have been stunning in their contemporary setting: "Man-maid, begone!"[10] The theatre at this moment in 1632 calls into question the whole culture of the naturalized transvestite actor. It is not irrelevant that Circe, the sorceress who transforms men into beasts, is the villain of this fable; but in fact the question she raises was increasingly central to Caroline theatrical life. Sophie Tomlinson points out that the word "actress" as a term for a stage player was first used of Queen Henrietta Maria in her court plays; Tomlinson persuasively argues that it was through the continuing acrimonious debate over women on the Whitehall stage that the naturalization of the actress took place. When the theatres reopened in 1660, the introduction of women on the public stage was accomplished without objection.[11]

What, then, about the claim that English moral attitudes precluded the appearance of women on the stage? Once again, the evidence concerning moral attitudes needs a hard look. The polemics of antitheatrical tracts are luridly misogynistic, but they hardly constitute evidence. Thomas Coryat's observation that in Venetian theatres he "saw women acte, a thing that I never saw before" is frequently cited, though the rest of the sentence, that he has "heard that it hath been sometimes used in London," is generally omitted.[12] No doubt Coryat is telling the truth about his own experience, but how far can we generalize from this? We know, for example, that Italian companies performed in Elizabethan England from time to time, and Italian companies always included women; was it really women Coryat had never seen on stage, or only professional actresses, or only English professional actresses? It may certainly have been the first of these, but we are not justified in assuming, therefore, either that because Coryat did not see women on stage in England, he could not have done so, or that because Coryat did not see them, nobody did.

G. E. Bentley cites the visit of a French company in 1629, at a time when Queen Henrietta Maria's amateur theatricals had already begun at court. A contemporary account of it survives in a letter of Thomas Brande's:

you should know, that last daye certaine vagrant French players, who had beene expelled from their owne contrey, *and those women*, did attempt, thereby giving just offence to all vertuous and well-disposed persons in this town, to act a certain lacivious and unchaste comedye, in the French tonge at the Blackfryers. Glad I am to saye they were hissed, hooted, and pippin-pelted from the stage, so as I do not thinke they will soone be ready to trie the same againe.[13]

This seems to justify all the usual generalizations about English moral attitudes; but in fact it only reveals the problems of using contemporary comment as evidence: as Bentley goes on to point out, the letter is seriously in error. The players performed publicly twice more during the next few weeks, at the Red Bull and the Fortune. Indeed, William Prynne gives a quite contradictory account of the occasion, noting with outrage the popularity of the "*French-women Actors*, in a Play not long since personated in *Blackefriers Play-house*, to which there was great resort."[14]

It is clear, then, that foreign actresses were acceptable on the

English public stage, at least from time to time. What about English actresses? Mistress Shepard appeared in a court performance; if she was a professional, this can hardly have been her only employment. We know that the famous Moll Frith, the model for Middleton's and Dekker's *The Roaring Girl*, gave a solo performance at the Fortune in 1611. I shall return to this; here, it is sufficient to point out that she did so at a major London theatre before an audience that bought tickets to see her, and without interference from the authorities. Nor was this a unique instance: Richard Madox recorded that in 1583 he "went to the theatre to see a scurvie play set out al by one virgin" – the actress pleased him no better than the play, and he left before the end.[15] How special are these cases?

An even more striking example relating to popular attitudes is found in the famous case of Richard Vennar's phantom play *England's Joy*. Vennar was a theatrical entrepreneur, clearly of considerable ingenuity. In 1602 he advertised a pageant play to be performed at the Swan celebrating English history and culminating in the reign of Queen Elizabeth – it is she who is England's joy. All that survives of the play is the playbill, which includes a detailed summary of the action; the crucial evidence for our purposes, however, comes from John Chamberlain, who wrote to Dudley Carleton that the major attraction of the production was that the roles were to be "acted only by certain gentlemen and gentlewomen of account."[16] The promise of seeing both women and gentry on stage sold a large number of tickets; but when the time came, Vennar was found to have decamped with the receipts, and there was no play – and doubtless never had been one.

If advertising women performers was an effective way of selling tickets, public opinion was obviously not averse to such a spectacle. Chambers cites two other examples of actresses on the Elizabethan stage, calling them exceptions that prove the rule;[17] but by this time it is clear that we do not at all know what the rule is. Obviously our evidence does not support any blanket claim that women were

8

excluded from the stages of Renaissance England, but it may certainly indicate that the culture, and the history that descends from it, had an interest in rendering them unnoticeable. Our own history, constructing gender and the nature of the desire engendered by it as a binary opposition, has rendered the constructed quality of the subject – what is recognized as masculine and feminine, whether on stage or off – all but invisible. This is a book about what has been unnoticeable and invisible.

2

The performance of desire

I have begun by questioning some basic information about the
English Renaissance theatre. It is a commonplace to observe that the
stage in Shakespeare's time was an exclusively male preserve, but
theatre historians tend to leave the matter there, as if the fact merely
constituted a practical arrangement and had no implications.[1] But it
has very broad implications, which are both cultural and specifically
sexual: the male public theatre represents a uniquely English solution
to the universal European disapproval of actresses. No contemporary
continental public theatre restricted the stage to men. So the first
puzzle, if one is looking at English Renaissance theatre in a European
context, is why this seemed a satisfactory arrangement to the English
and not to anyone else.

Secondly, I have problematized the fact of a male theatre in
England, pointing out that the claim of an all-male public stage at
the very least needs some serious qualification. But even where the
stage was a male preserve, as it certainly was in the commercial
theatrical companies of Renaissance England, the t'.eatre was not.
The theatre was a place of unusual freedom for women in the
period; foreign visitors comment on the fact that English women go
to theatre unescorted and unmasked, and a large proportion of the
audience consisted of women. The puzzle here would be why a
culture that so severely regulated the lives of women in every other
sphere suspended its restrictions in the case of theatre. The fact of
the large female audience must have had important consequences for
the development of English popular drama. It meant that the success

of any play was significantly dependent on the receptiveness of women; and this in turn means that theatrical representations – whether of women or men or anything else – also depended for their success to a significant degree on the receptiveness of women. When we see dramatic depictions of women in Elizabethan drama that we consider degrading, it has become common to explain the fact by declaring them to be male fantasies, and to point to the exclusively male stage to account for them. But this cannot be correct: theatres are viable only insofar as they satisfy their audiences. The depictions must at the very least represent *cultural* fantasies, and women are implicated in them as well as men.[2]

Next, as I have indicated, it is in an important respect not quite true even to say that the English public stage was exclusively male. At least up to the 1530s there were public peformances of various kinds – civic pageants and guild plays – that demonstrably did include women. Elizabethan theatrical companies contained no women, but Italian troupes, which were family affairs and always included women, visited England from time to time and performed not only at court but throughout the country. When such performances took place in conjunction with royal progresses, and therefore under the queen's patronage, theatre became an extension of the court; and it may be relevant that on these occasions the theatre that included women would have been associated with the royal presence. Elizabeth's England, then, did in fact from time to time see women on the professional stage. What they apparently did not see was *English* women on the professional stage: the distinction they maintained was not between men and women but between "us" and "them" – what was appropriate for foreigners was not appropriate for the English, and women on display became increasingly associated with Roman Catholicism.

We can tell something about how the gender question was regarded by asking whether women are seen in English Renaissance plays as "them" rather than "us," as the Other. A case can certainly be made for this: there is a large component of male bonding in Shakespeare, what Eve Sedgwick calls the homosocial; and plays like *The Merry Wives of Windsor* and *Othello* certainly have powerful elements of the men against the women, though it is not at all clear, if we think of these plays in this way, who are "us" and who are "them" – the men in *The Merry Wives* lose hands down to the women, and the profound ambivalences of gender relationships have always proved notoriously disturbing to audiences in *Othello*.[3] Emilia on the relationships between the sexes

> 'Tis not a year or two shows us a man.
> They are all but stomachs and we all but food;
> They eat us hungerly, and when they are full,
> They belch us   (3.4.103–6)

or,

> jealous souls will not be answered so;
> They are not ever jealous for the cause,
> But jealous for they're jealous   (159–61)

certainly is not speaking as an outsider. In the context of *Othello*, this is the normative view, the one we are expected to agree with. But in a larger sense we would have to say that there are lots of Others, and Others of many kinds, in this theatre; in fact, Elizabethan drama is often dependent on otherness. Comedies are Italian, French or provincial, tragedies Spanish or Scandinavian or ancient; pastorals programmatically take place Somewhere Else. Dekker, Jonson and Middleton, placing comedies in contemporary London, are recognized as doing something new. The Other, for this theatre, is as much foreign as female – in their separate ways, both Othello and Portia are the Other. And in the largest sense, such figures are metonyms for theatre itself, the great Other functioning within society as both a threat and a refuge.[4]

But just as theatre is an Other that comes from and expresses the self, so the women of the Renaissance stage must be as much emanations of that self as the men are. Male and female are often presented within Renaissance culture as a binary opposition, opposites and complements; but how different are women from men? The difficulty of locating the differences is the subject of a wooing scene in George Wilkins' play *The Miseries of Enforced Marriage* (1607). A shy suitor named Scarborrow is engaged in his first interview with Clare, the woman he hopes to marry. Assuming that she will begin the conversation, he is disconcerted by her silence, which he registers as unfeminine:

SCAR. Prithee tell me: are you not a woman?
CLARE. I know not that neither, till I am better acquainted with a man.
SCAR. And how would you be acquainted with a man?
CLARE. To distinguish betwixt himself and myself.
SCAR. Why, I am a man.
CLARE. That's more than I know, sir.
SCAR. To approve that I am no less, thus I kiss thee.
CLARE. And by that proof I am a man too, for I have kissed you.[5]

The moment is parodic, but the joke depends on a truth: women are defined in this culture by their relation to men, yet the distinctions of gender are fluid and unclear.

Renaissance women are often described as commodities, whose marriages are arranged for the advantage or convenience of men, either their fathers, or the male authority figures in their and their prospective husbands' families. This is correct as far as it goes, but it does not distinguish women from men: alliances were normally arranged for sons just as for daughters – the distinction here is between fathers or guardians and children, not between the sexes; Early Modern England was a patriarchal society. Fantasies of freedom in Shakespeare tend to take the form of escapes from the tyranny of elders to a world where the children can make their own society, which usually means where they can arrange their own marriages – and thereby enjoy the benefits of the patriarchal structure, rather than suffer its liabilities. Whether this is conceived as ultimately benign and restorative, as in *A Midsummer Night's Dream, As You Like It, Twelfth Night, The Winter's Tale*, or disastrous, as in *Othello* and *Romeo and Juliet*, it works for women as well as men: the crucial element is the restrictive father, elder brother, guardian, not the sex of the child. Once on their own, Rosalind and Orlando, Lorenzo and Jessica are free to choose each other; whereas Bertram's marriage to Helena is no less constrained than the one proposed for Juliet to the County Paris. The problem is the father or the king or the structure of authority, not one's gender.

This is not to say that it is not preferable to be male in the Renaissance world: obviously it is; and though the women of Shakespearean comedy generally get what they want, the happy endings of *As You Like It* and *The Merchant of Venice* nevertheless promise significantly greater benefits to Orlando, Bassanio and Lorenzo than to their wives. Rosalind and Portia, for all their ingenuity, wit and charm, represent for their impecunious husbands not merely good conversation but place and fortune, and Jessica is all too openly equated with the money Lorenzo acquires with her. Would any of these marriages have constituted a happy ending had the wife not been rich? The defeat of patriarchy, in such cases, results only in its replication; it is to the point that the sole option imagined by the young in their quest for freedom is marriage – this is all that freedom permits, the transformation of the son into another patriarch. But the advantages of maleness in the culture as a whole were neither unqualified nor constant (they were considerably smaller for sons than for their fathers, and smaller still for younger sons than for the eldest); nor was patriarchy single and uninflected: the patriarchy of husbands conflicted with the patriarchy of fathers and elder brothers, and the patriarchy of the church and of the crown conflicted with both.

Let us consider gender issues in relation to generational issues. *The Winter's Tale* includes a particularly subversive version of that fantasy of freedom, the return to childhood. Leontes, after his first flash of violent jealousy, explains his distracted manner to Hermione and Polixenes in this way:

> Looking on the lines
> Of my boy's face, methoughts I did recoil
> Twenty-three years, and saw myself unbreeched,
> In my green velvet coat, my dagger muzzled,
> Lest it should bite its master, and so prove,
> As ornaments oft do, too dangerous. (1.2.153–8)

The return to childhood is represented as a retreat from sexuality and the dangers of manhood exemplified in unmuzzled daggers. Leontes sees himself "unbreeched," not yet in breeches: Elizabethan children of both sexes were dressed in skirts until the age of seven or so; the "breeching" of boys was the formal move out of the common gender of childhood, which was both female in appearance and largely controlled by women, and into the world of men. This event was traditionally the occasion for a significant family ceremony.

The childhood world to which Leontes imagines himself returning has been described by his royal guest and inseparable childhood friend Polixenes as both Edenic and presexual:

> We were as twinned lambs that did frisk i'th'sun
> And bleat the one at th'other; what we changed
> Was innocence for innocence; we knew not
> The doctrine of ill-doing, nor dreamed
> That any did; had we pursued that life,
> And our weak spirits ne'er been higher reared
> With stronger blood, we should have answered heaven

> Boldly "not guilty," the imposition cleared
> Hereditary ours.

It is a world without vice or temptation, in which even original sin appears to have been dealt with. Significantly, there are no women in it, only the best friend, an emotional twin.

At this point Leontes' queen Hermione enters the fantasy with a pertinent observation:

> By this we gather
> You have tripped since.

Polixenes agrees; the fall from grace is a fall into sexuality:

> O my most sacred lady,
> Temptations have been born to 's, for
> In those unfledged days was my wife a girl;
> Your precious self had not yet crossed the eyes
> Of my young playfellow.

Hermione both protests and concurs:

> Of this make no conclusion, lest you say
> Your queen and I are devils. Yet go on,
> Th'offences we have made you do we'll answer,
> If you first sinned with us, and that with us
> You did continue fault, and that you slipped not
> With any but with us.   (1.2.66–86)

However good-natured their banter, Hermione's projected conclusion is the logical one: "your queen and I are devils." Her teasing view of marriage as a continuing state of sin with diabolical agents repeats the view of sexuality implicit in the men's fantasy.

It is a fantasy that is critical to the play, a determining feature of the subsequent tragic action. Critics for two hundred years have declared Leontes' paranoid jealousy inexplicable, but within the context of that dream of what it means to be a child, Leontes' behavior is not only understandable, it is in a way inevitable. No

16

particular word or gesture is required to trigger Leontes' paranoid jealousy; the translation of the inseparable friend into the dangerous rival, and of the chaste wife into a whore, is implicit in the fantasy, its worst-case scenario, so to speak, replicating the situation Shakespeare had imagined with such detailed intensity in the Dark Lady sonnets. This is the consequence of women entering the world of male friendship. And when Leontes retreats from it he is retreating not only from women and sex: he is retreating from his place in one of the very few normative families in Shakespeare – families consisting of father, mother and children. Most families in Shakespeare have only one parent; the very few that include both parents generally have only one child, and when that configuration appears, it tends to be presented, as Leontes' marriage is presented, as exceedingly dangerous to the child: consider Juliet and her parents, Macduff and Lady Macduff, Coriolanus and Virgilia, Imogen with Cymbeline and his queen, the Duke and Duchess of York arguing about whether to denounce their son as a traitor. It is a configuration that, with the single exception of the Page family in *The Merry Wives of Windsor*, never appears in comedy.

Marriage is a dangerous condition in Shakespeare. We are always told that comedies end in marriages, and that this is normative. A few of Shakespeare's do, but the much more characteristic Shakespearean conclusion comes just before the marriage, and sometimes, as in *Love's Labour's Lost* and *Twelfth Night*, with an entirely unexpected delay or postponement. Plays that continue beyond the point where comedy ends, with the old fogies defeated and a happy marriage successfully concluded, depict the condition as utterly disastrous: *Romeo and Juliet, Othello.* Perhaps this is really the Shakespearean norm. Most Shakespearean marriages of longer duration are equally disheartening, with shrewishness, jealousy and manipulativeness the norm in comedy, and real destructiveness in tragedy: Oberon and Titania; the Merry Wives; Capulet and Lady Capulet; Hotspur and his wife; Claudius and Gertrude; Macbeth and Lady Macbeth; Cymbeline and his queen; Postumus and Imogen; Antigonus and Paulina. The open, trusting marriage of Brutus and Portia is all but unique in Shakespeare; the love of Macbeth and Lady Macbeth eventuates in female domination and effeminacy in a world where witchcraft is naturalized; and the only Shakespearean marriage that is presented specifically as sexually happy is that of Claudius and Gertrude, the incestuous union of a murderer and an adulteress. This is the dark side of the culture's institutionalization of marriage and patriarchy – what is striking is how little of the bright side Shakespeare includes. All the fun is in the wooing; what happens after marriage, between husbands and wives, parents and children, is a subject for tragedy.

In fact, loving relationships between men and women interest Shakespeare intensely, but not, on the whole, as husbands and wives. We might go on to say not even invariably as men and women: a significant group of plays require the woman to become a man for the wooing to be effected. The dangers of women in erotic situations, whatever they may be, can be disarmed by having the women play men, just as in the theatre the dangers of women on the stage (whatever *they* may be) can be disarmed by having men play the women. The interchangeability of the sexes is, on both the fictive and the material level, an assumption of this theatre.

What then is the difference between the sexes? On Shakespeare's stage it is a difference we would regard as utterly superficial, a matter of costumes and mannerisms; nevertheless, the superficies produce a difference that is absolute – gender disguises in this theatre are represented as all but impenetrable.[6] Indeed, the convention remains as powerful in the theatre of *Some Like It Hot* and *Tootsie* as in that of *Twelfth Night* and *Epicoene*. How relevant are the conventions of theatrical gender to those of culture and physiology? For us, they would seem to be hardly relevant at all: without the extra layer of travesty provided by the boy actor, the figure beneath the costume is the real thing – the whole point of the cross-dressing in *Some Like It Hot* and *Tootsie* is precisely for the audience to see through the impersonation, though the characters cannot. Ours is a theatre of named, known, and (most important for the purposes of this argument) gendered actors; to be seriously deceived by cross-gendered disguising is for us deeply disturbing, the stuff of classic horror movies like *Psycho*. We want to believe that the question of gender is settled, biological, controlled by issues of sexuality, and we claim to be quite clear about which sex is which – our genital organs, those inescapable facts, preclude any ultimate ambiguity. Hence, in Neil Jordan's *The Crying Game*, Jaye Davidson's impeccable femininity was demolished in an instant by the display of his penis, and after this point in the film he wore only male clothing ("for protection," as the film equivocally put it; but whose protection, his or ours?) A crucial element in the role was the fact that this was Jaye Davidson's first film – ambiguously named, he could play the role because he was totally unknown, which in this case means specifically that the sex of this actor was unknown. Sex for us is the bottom line, the ultimate truth of gender.

Or so we claim. Nevertheless, a modern father who urges his timid son to "be a man" is perfectly comprehensible, despite the fact that this commonplace exhortation assumes that masculinity is achieved not through biology but through an effort of will. We are fully the heirs of the Renaissance in this: Early Modern moralists continually reminded their charges that manhood was not a natural condition but a quality to be striven for and maintained only through constant vigilance, and even then with the utmost difficulty. There has always been a crucial behavioral element to gender that has nothing to do with the organs of generation.[7]

But for Renaissance physiology, even the distinction of the sexes could be blurred, sometimes frighteningly so. Gynecological treatises offered widely variant accounts of the etiology of gender, often concurrently and without any determination as to their relative likelihood, but the most persistent line of medical and anatomical thought from the time of Galen had cited homologies in the genital structure of the sexes to show that male and female were versions of the same unitary species.[8] In this view of sexuality, the female genitals were simply the male genitals inverted, and carried internally rather than externally. Sexual experience was conceived to be the same in both; during coitus, both not only experience orgasm but ejaculate, and female ejaculation with its component of female seed is just as necessary for conception as male ejaculation is. Both male and female seeds are present in every fetus; a fetus becomes male rather than female if the male seed is dominant, and generates enough heat to press the genital organs outward – if, that is, the fetus is stronger, with strength being conceived as heat.[9]

In this version of anatomical history, we all begin as female, and masculinity is a development out of and away from femininity.[10] Logically, therefore, the medical literature from Roman times onward confirms the theory by recording numerous cases of women completing the physiological process and turning into men under the pressure of some great exertion or excitement. The sixteenth-century physician Ambroise Paré's version of the thesis includes several modern cases. The most famous and recent, a shepherd named Germain Garnier, had been a woman named Marie until the age of fifteen, at which time, as she was chasing her pigs, her genitals turned inside out, transforming her from female to male.[11] Garnier was still alive in Montaigne's time, and though the story in Paré is presented as a case of simple physiology, Montaigne saw more than anatomy in it and used it as an example in his essay *Of the Power of the Imagination*. He is cagey about whether he actually met Garnier, though from an entry in his travel journal for 1580 it is clear that he did not,[12] but he briefly describes the man ("heavily bearded, and old, and not married"), and summarizes his history and the townspeople's accounts of him. The essayist's attitude toward the story is characteristically detached, but nothing in it suggests that he

20

considers Garnier a fraud or doubts the authenticity of the transformation. Indeed, he has no difficulty naturalizing it, observing that "this sort of accident is frequently met with."[13]

Helkiah Crooke, whose *Mikrokosmographia* (1615) was the most compendious English synthesis of Renaissance anatomical knowledge, provides a striking testimony to the ambiguities of the science of gender in the period. Writing for an audience of physicians, Crooke presents a detailed discussion of the homological sex thesis, which he accepts with minor reservations, and then follows it with an entirely contradictory thesis in which women are not inverted versions of men at all, but are genuinely different and have their own kind of perfection, providing the human animal with substance and nurture, as the male provides it with form. Both theories have a long history of authority behind them; both derive ultimately from Aristotle, though the homological argument was associated principally with Galen.[14] Thus, in a chapter on the male genitals, Crooke explains women as incomplete men: "the Testicles in Men are larger, and of a hotter nature then in Women . . .; heat abounding in men thrusts them forth of the body, whereas in women they remain within, because their dull and sluggish heat is not sufficient to thrust them out," concluding that "the truth of this appeareth by manifold stories of such Women, whose more active and more operative heat have thrust out their Testicles, and of Women made them Men."[15] Ten pages later, introducing his discourse on the female genitals, Crooke is rhapsodic on the divine wisdom of anatomical homology:

a woman is so much less perfect then a man by how much her heat is less and weaker then his; yet . . . is this imperfection turned unto perfection, because without the woman, mankind could not have been perfected by the perfecter sex.[16]

But fifty pages farther on Crooke is flatly denying the homology of male and female organs: "We must not think that the female is an imperfect male differing only in the position of the genitals."[17] Galen to the contrary notwithstanding, dissection shows that the clitoris differs significantly from the penis, "neither is there . . . any similitude between the bottom of the womb inverted, and the scrotum." As for the confirmatory stories of sudden sex change, he now declares "all of them monstrous" – that is, factual but not part of any normal process – "and some not credible."[18]

The ambiguity is in no way unusual in the period, nor is the fact that Crooke sees no need to reconcile the conflicting scientific arguments. He has, in effect, one theory when his attention is focused on men, another when it is focused on women; the latter, though it contradicts and, indeed, to post-Enlightenment eyes ought to preclude the former, does not, in Crooke's account, negate or even supersede it. The empirical evidence of dissection, which serves as the clinching argument in his account of the female condition, does not impinge in the slightest on his account of the male: the relevance of evidence is a function of the thesis being argued, not the other way round. Modern readers faced with so unambiguous a pronouncement as "all of them monstrous and some not credible" will doubtless want to insist that Crooke cannot have, a few pages earlier, really believed in "the truth . . . of women made . . . men." But Renaissance arguments rarely work in a way that seems to us neat and logical. Both theories are authoritative, each has its utility in explicating some part of the subject; each is produced not in the abstract, as part of a synthesis of gender theory, but at the appropriate moment in a discussion of physiology and behavior.

In the same way Sir Thomas Browne, like Crooke a practicing physician, was on the one hand empirically persuaded of the absolute distinction between the sexes. He writes in *Christian Morals* that "Men and Women have their proper Virtues and Vices, and even Twins of different sexes have not only distinct coverings in the Womb, but differing qualities and Virtuous Habits after"; and this leads him to a plea to maintain the separation of the genders in society: "transplace not their Proprieties and confound not their Distinctions."[19] In *Pseudodoxia Epidemica* he asserts that his empirical knowledge of anatomy has convinced him that Galen was wrong about the male and female organs being inverted versions of each other, "the testicles being so seated in the female, that they admit not of protrusion; and the neck of the matrix wanting those parts which are discoverable in the organ of virility."[20]

Against this utter conviction of the integrity and immutability of the genders, however, we find the equally complete assurance of this passage from the same chapter of *Pseudodoxia Epidemica*:

As for the mutation of sexes, or transition into one another, we cannot deny it in Hares, it being observable in Man. For hereof beside Empedocles or Tiresias, there are not a few examples: and though very few, or rather none which have emasculated or turned into women, yet very many who from an esteem or reality of being women have infallibly proved Men . . . And that not only mankind, but many other Animals may suffer this transexion, we will not deny, or hold it at all impossible.

Beside this paragraph Browne has placed the marginal gloss, "Transmutation of Sexes, viz. of Women into Men, granted."[21]

Granted! Women are totally different from men from before the moment of birth, even in the womb, and their genital organs "admit not of protrusion," yet the possibility of their transformation into men goes without saying. The only sticking point is the question of whether the process can be reversed, and men turn into women; it is this that is judiciously declared to be, if not impossible, at least so rare as to be negligible (there are "very few, or rather none"). Those transformations that are attested to as scientific fact only work in one direction, from female to male, which is conceived to be upward, toward completion. But these are for Browne, as for Montaigne, Ambroise Paré, and much of the time for Helkiah Crooke, facts.

As for the other part of Helkiah Crooke's convictions about gender, in which women are not versions of men but develop in their own way and are equally complete beings, it sounds like a blow for freedom, but for all its air of empiricism and modern good sense, it is no more advanced scientifically than the homological theory: both ultimately derive their authority from Aristotle, and the crucial empirical evidence comes not from Crooke's own dissections, but from the reports of the French anatomist André du Laurens, one of his principal modern sources – the account is carefully and frequently punctuated with the parenthetical "(saith Laurentius)"; Crooke is only rarely bold enough to venture a "methinks." It is clear that this is a scientist for whom authority weighs a great deal more heavily than empiricism. In any case, the denial of female imperfection implied little that was beneficial to women within the structures of Renaissance authority; women were still, by nature, firmly ensconced below men in the hierarchy. Throughout the age, and despite the increasing evidence provided by the study of anatomy, outside the professional scientific community homology remained the predominant theory – as, for example, in *The Roaring Girl* the transvestite Moll Cutpurse is accounted for by explaining that "her birth began / Ere she was all made": both her femininity and her desire to be male are functions of her incompleteness.[22]

Needless to say, the persistence of homology has little to do with science. Renaissance ideology had a vested interest in defining women in terms of men; the aim is thereby to establish the parameters of maleness, not of womanhood. This is why Crooke abandons the homological thesis when he turns to the specifics of the female anatomy; to define the nature of women, it is not useful. As we have seen, the scientific truth or falsehood of either theory is not at issue – the two claims are parts of two different arguments, and they are not in competition. All such claims, of course, are not merely scientific, but imply (like the scientific claims of all eras including our own) a political agenda. The homology cited from Galen onward is only anatomical; the notion that women are versions of men is no more egalitarian than the notion that women are anatomically independent. Most of the scholastic opinion codified by Ian Maclean in *The Renaissance Notion of Women* assumes the correctness of the homological thesis, but nevertheless stresses the differences between men and women, not their similarities, and these are invariably prejudicial. Women are less intelligent, more passionate, less in control of their affections, and so forth. The difference in degree of perfection becomes in practical terms a powerful difference in kind, and the homological arguments are used to justify the whole range of male domination over women. Subjectivity, in this line of reasoning, is always masculine – indeed, Judith Butler observes that the binary opposition of male and female is "itself a ruse for the monologic elaboration of the masculine."[23]

The frightening part of the teleology for the Renaissance mind, however, is precisely the fantasy of its reversal, the "very few, or rather none" of Sir Thomas Browne: the conviction that men can turn into – or be turned into – women; or perhaps more exactly, can be turned *back* into women, losing the strength that enabled the male potential to be realized in the first place. In this version of the medical literature we all start as women, and the culture confirmed this by dressing all children in skirts until the age of seven or so, when the boy, as Leontes recalls, was "breeched," or put into pants, removed from the care of women, and began to be trained as a man.[24] From this point on, for a man to associate with women was felt to be increasingly dangerous – not only for the woman, but even more for the man: lust effeminates, makes men incapable of manly pursuits; hence the pervasive antithesis of love and war. Thomas Wright, in *The Passions of the Mind in General*, warning against the dangers of love, writes that "a personable body is often linked with a pestilent soul; a valiant Captain in the field for the most part is infected with an effeminate affection at home."[25] The effeminate affection is his passion for women; similarly Romeo, berating himself for his unwillingness to harm Tybalt, cries out,

> O sweet Juliet,
> Thy beauty hath made me effeminate,
> And in my temper softened valor's steel!   (3.1.118–20).

Such formulations are all but axiomatic in the period, and the word "effeminate," over and over, serves the basic explanatory function in them. Women are dangerous to men because sexual passion for women renders men effeminate: this is an age in which sexuality itself is misogynistic, as the love of women threatens the integrity of the perilously achieved male identity. Robert Burton elucidates the matter with uncharacteristic directness: love is "full of fear, anxiety, doubt, care, peevishness, suspicion, it turns a man into a woman."[26] The fear of effeminization is a central element in all discussions of what constitutes a "real man" in the period, and the fantasy of the reversal of the natural transition from woman to man underlies it. It also, in a much more clearly pathological way, underlies the standard arguments against the stage in antitheatrical tracts from the time of the Church Fathers on. In this context, the very institution of theatre is a threat to manhood and the stability of the social hierarchy, as unescorted women and men without their wives socialize freely, and (it follows) flirt with each other and take each other off to bed: the association of theatre with sex is absolutely pervasive in these polemics.

But in England, the sexuality feared is more subversive than even this suggests, precisely because of the transvestism of the stage. It is argued first that the boys who perform the roles of women will be transformed into their roles and play the part in reality. This claim has its basis in a Platonic argument, but in the Puritan tracts it merges with a general fear of blurred social and sexual boundaries, of roles and costumes adulterating the essences that God has given us. Jonas Barish, in his exhaustive and indispensable study of the antitheatrical material, relates the hostility to transvestite actors to the synchronous revival of medieval sumptuary laws, the attempt to prevent members of one social class from appearing to be members of another (thus tradesmen were enjoined from wearing silk), and he quotes William Perkins to the effect that "wanton and excessive apparel . . . maketh a confusion of such degrees and callings as God hath ordained." "Distinctions of dress," Barish comments, "however external and theatrical they may seem to us, for Perkins virtually belong to our essence, and may no more be tampered with than that essence itself."[27] This is certainly the way the polemicists view the situation; but it is precisely the essence that is the problem. What *is* our God-given essence, that it can be transformed by the clothes we wear? Philip Stubbes, in a passage that bears directly on the question of transvestite actors, deplores a current (and recurrent) fashion of masculine dress for women. "Our apparel," he says, "was given us as a sign distinctive to discern betwixt sex and sex, and therefore one to wear the apparel of another sex is to participate with the same, and to adulterate the verity of his own kind. Wherefore these women may not improperly be called *Hermaphroditi,* that is, monsters of both kinds, half women, half men."[28] It is the fragility, the radical instability of our essence, that is assumed here, and the metamorphic quality of our sinful nature. The enormous popularity of Ovid in the age reflects both its desires and its deepest fears.

But the argument against transvestite actors warns of an even more frightening metamorphosis than the transformation of the boy into a monster of both kinds. Male spectators, it is argued, will be seduced by the impersonation, and losing their reason will become effeminate, which in this case means not only that they will lust after the woman in the drama, which is bad enough, but also after the youth beneath the woman's costume, thereby playing the woman's role themselves. This fear, which has been brilliantly anatomized by Laura Levine,[29] is so pervasive in the tracts, and so unlike modern kinds of sexual anxiety, that it is worth pausing over.

John Rainoldes says the adoption by men of women's clothing incites a lust that is specifically homoerotic:

what sparkles of lust to that vice the putting of women's attire on men may kindle in unclean affections, as Nero showed in Sporus, Heliogabalus in himself; yea certain, who grew not to such excess of impudency, yet arguing the same in causing their boys to wear long hair like women.

Scripture, he continues, condemns prostitution of both women and men, "detesting specially the male by terming him a *dog*," and concludes by urging that we "control likewise the means and occasions whereby men are transformed into dogs, the sooner to cut off all incitements to that beastly filthiness, or rather more than beastly."[30] Marginal glosses refer the reader to biblical and classical instances of sodomy, homosexual sadism and homosexual marriage. The slippage here from effeminacy to bestiality is notable, and should remind us that in this culture femininity is not equated with docility – on the contrary, what is feared in women is their violent and uncontrollable appetites.

Subsequently, citing the authority of Socrates, Rainoldes compares the homoerotic response engendered by transvestite boys to the sting of poisonous spiders: "if they do but touch men only with their mouth, they put them to wonderful pain and make them mad: so beautiful boys by kissing do sting and pour secretly in a kind of poison."[31] Here the attraction of men to beautiful boys is treated as axiomatic. But this in fact is only the prelude to a much more vehement tirade against the universal sexuality evoked by theatre, a lust not distinguished by the gender of its object:

can wise men be persuaded that there is no wantonness in the players' parts when experience showeth (as wise men have observed) that men are made adulterers and enemies of all chastity by coming to such plays? that senses are moved, affections are delighted, hearts though strong and constant are vanquished by such players? that an effeminate stage-player, while he faineth love, imprinteth wounds of love?

The effeminate stage player here is the agent of a universal effeminacy. William Prynne goes a step farther, localizing and particularizing the sexuality. In *Histriomastix* the transvestitism of the stage is especially dangerous because female dress is an important stimulant specifically to homoeroticism: the "male priests of Venus" satisfy their companions, the "passive beastly sodomites in Florida," by wearing women's clothes, the "better to elicit, countenance, act and color their unnatural execrable uncleannesses."[32] Heterosexuality here only provides the fetish that enables the true homosexual response to emerge. It is significant that the transvestite is not the passive one in this relationship.

Rainoldes, Prynne and any number of other antitheatrical writers offer observations such as these as models for the theatrical experience. For such writers, the very fact that women are prohibited from the stage reveals the true etiology of theatre: what the spectator is "really" attracted to in plays is an undifferentiated sexuality, a sexuality that does not distinguish men from women and reduces men to women – the deepest fear in antitheatrical tracts, far deeper than the fear that women in the audience will become whores, is the fear of a universal effeminization. In this anxiety, the fact of transvestite boys is really only incidental; it is the whole concept of the mimetic art that is at issue, the art itself that effeminates. The growth of desire through the experience of theatre is a sinister progression: the play excites the spectator, and sends him home to "perform" himself; the result is sexual abandon with one's wife, or more often with any available woman (all women at the playhouse being considered available), or worst of all, the spectator begins by lusting after a female character, but ends by having sex with the man she "really" is. Philip Stubbes gives a particularly clear statement of this anxiety: "the fruits of plays and interludes" are, he says, that after theatre, "everyone brings another homeward of their way very friendly, and in their secret conclaves, covertly, they play the sodomites or worse."[33] The sodomites in this case are probably not homoerotic, since Stubbes elsewhere in the tract uses sodomy to refer to heterosexual fornication – though this may be giving

Stubbes too much credit for consistency, a quality not otherwise much in evidence in the work. Jonathan Goldberg argues persuasively, however, that homosexual activity is well beyond the power of Stubbes' imagination.[34] But Prynne takes the logical next step, citing this passage as a proof of the specifically homoerotic character of the stage:

Yea, witness . . . M. Stubbes, his *Anatomy of Abuses* . . . where he affirms that players and play-haunters in their secret conclaves play the sodomites; together with some modern examples of such, who have been desperately enamored with players' boys thus clad in woman's apparel, so far as to solicit them by words, by letters, even actually to abuse them . . . This I have heard credibly reported of a scholar of Bailliol College, and I doubt not but it may be verified of divers others.[35]

The assumption here is first that the basic form of response to theatre is erotic, second that erotically, theatre is uncontrollably exciting, and third, that the basic, essential form of erotic excitement in men is homosexual – that indeed, women are only a cover for men. And though the assumption as Prynne articulates it is clearly pathological, a *reductio ad absurdum* of antitheatrical commonplaces, it is also clearly related both to all the generalized anxieties attendant upon the institutionalization of masculinity within the culture, and to the sanctioned homoeroticism that played so large a role in relationships between men.

3

The eye of the beholder

But is there anything correct about Prynne's analysis? What did audiences see when they went to theatre, the female character or the boy beneath the dress? Peter Stallybrass emphasizes precisely the indeterminacy of the transvestite stage, observing that it "resists the sexual and narrative teleologies which would be developed in the eighteenth and nineteenth centuries," but goes on to find in it "less a matter of indeterminacy than of the production of contrary fixations: the imagined body of a woman, the staged body of a boy actor, the material presence of clothes."[1] Testimony from the period, sparse as it is, is contradictory in just the ways that Stallybrass suggests. In a well known passage from *Urania*, Lady Mary Wroth implies that the consciousness of the boy beneath the costume is both controlling and anerotic. In an episode in the romance, a lover sees his mistress "with all passionate ardency, seeke and sue for the stranger's love; yet he unmoveable, was no further wrought, than if he had seene a delicate play-boy acte a loving woman part, and knowing him a boy, lik'd only his action."[2] Wroth's assumption (to which I shall return) is precisely the opposite of Rainoldes' and Prynne's: that the stage's transvestism works to insulate it from lustful feelings, not to arouse them. Thomas Heywood, in one of the very few English defenses of the stage, agrees that audiences are always aware they are not watching women:

To see our youths attired in the habit of women, who knowes not what their intents be? who cannot distinguish them by their names, assuredly, knowing they are but to represent such a Lady, at such a time appoynted.[3]

But on the other hand, he argues in favor of history plays that their audiences react to "the person of any bold English man presented . . . as if the Personator were the man Personated."[4] An Oxford scholar named Henry Jackson provides evidence that what Heywood says of the response to staged patriotic heroes is true of staged romantic women as well. Writing enthusiastically of a performance of *Othello* by the King's Men in 1610, he singles out for praise "Desdemona illa apud nos a marito occisa," "Desdemona killed before us by her husband":

although she always acted her whole part supremely well, yet when she was killed she was even more moving, for when she fell back upon the bed she implored the pity of the spectators by her very face.[5]

The original Latin is of course without pronouns, but the two past participles ("occisa," "interfecta") agree with a female Desdemona, not with the male actor. The boy here has disappeared; Desdemona as both actor and character is gendered female. The full ambiguity of contemporary attitudes is epitomized in Chapman's *May Day*, when Quintiliano proposes to Leonoro that they hire out Leonoro's boy as an actor:

Afore heaven, "tis a sweet-faced child, methinks he should show well in woman's attire . . . I'll help thee to three crowns a week for him, and she can act well. Hast ever practised, my pretty Ganymede? (3.3.228–33)

The mere mention of female attire genders the boy female, and the identification of the cross-dressing actor as Ganymede follows as logically as it does in any hysterical tract of Rainoldes and Prynne – or in *As You Like It*. There is, in fact, a precisely analogous moment in *As You Like It*, though editors have done their best to suppress it. Hymen, in the final moments of the play, presents Rosalind to her father:

> Good Duke receiue thy daughter,
> Hymen from heauen brought her,

Yea brought her hether.
That thou mightst ioyne his hand with his,
Whose heart within his bosome is.

This is the reading of the folio text. Since the third folio, however, "his hand" in the penultimate line has been regularly revised to read "her hand." But there is no reason to emend: Rosalind, still cross-dressed as Ganymede, is correctly gendered male.[6] Sixty years later, when Pepys went to see Edward Kynaston, the last of the great male heroines, the gender rules were still in force: "one Kynaston, a boy, acted the Duke's sister but made the loveliest lady that ever I saw in my life – only her voice not very good."[7]

Perhaps the most striking example of the dependence of gender on costume, and not on sexuality, is found in the romance that lies behind the cross-dressing of *Twelfth Night*, Barnabe Riche's tale of Apolonius and Silla. Silla, the Viola character, in her male disguise under the name of her twin brother Silvio, is accused of impregnating Julina, the Olivia figure, and is ordered by the duke to marry her or face death. The real culprit, of course, is her twin, who passing through the town on his travels was entertained by Julina, spent the night with her, and in conventional masculine fashion decamped the next day. Silla/Silvio, put to the final test of her gender, considers her (or in the circumstances, his) plight:

hearing an othe sworne so divinely that he had gotten a woman with childe, was like to beleeve that it had bin true in very deede; but remembryng his owne impediment, thought it impossible that he should committe suche an acte.

The degree of consideration Silla gives to Julina's accusation here is notable. She determines that a revelation of the truth is her only recourse:

And here with all loosing his garmentes doune to his stomacke, and shewed Julina his breastes and pretie teates, surmounting farre the whiteness of snow itself.[8]

33

Silla's gender is determined by Silla's garments, even in removing them.

The crux of all this, as Stallybrass suggests, is the costume, and costume remains a site of intense moral debate throughout the period. The argument that women's apparel in the theatre provides a cover for the homoerotic body is not unique to William Prynne. The notion that the transvestite stage is an enabling mechanism for homosexual activity is central to the extended confrontation between Rainoldes and William Gager over the performance of plays by Oxford undergraduates, arguably the most searching discussion of the subject in the age. Most of this has to do with interpretations of the relevant passage from Deuteronomy proscribing cross-dressing, but Rainoldes' charges are also more specific, and Gager is forced to deny that acting was in fact a cover for action:

As for the danger of kissinge bewtifull boyes, I knowe not howe this suspition shoulde reache to us, for it is untrwe . . . that owre Eurymachus did kisse owre Malantho. I have enquyred of the partyes themselves, whether any suche action was used by them, and thay constantly denye it; sure I ame, no suche thinge was taught.[9]

Both the vehemence of the charges and the fact that denials are felt to be necessary are evidence that there is a real cultural issue at stake here. Why, after all, should women's garments on men be considered a temptation to homosexuality? Dresses are concealing; it is the tights and codpieces of male apparel that are revealing and tempting. Concepts of sodomy in the antitheatrical discourse in fact depend on a heterosexual model; the act remains not merely unnameable, but inconceivable. Rainoldes at one point even makes the extraordinary argument that cross-dressing "is a great provocation of men to lust and leacherie: because a womans garment being put on a man doeth vehemently touch and move him with the remembrance and imagination of a woman; and the imagination of a thing desirable doth stirr up the desire."[10] There is no desire for men imagined here; what is elicited by travesty, the great danger, is heterosexual desire. Ironically, Rainoldes' and Prynne's fears point ahead to the time when actresses finally became normative on the English stage, and transvestite plots burgeoned, as they had done in Spain and France for sixty years. Cross-dressing provided much of the substance of drama for those societies that did *not* have transvestite theatres – men paid to see women in breeches and hose.

Why, then, if boys in women's dress are so threatening, did the English maintain a transvestite theatre? It is necessary to remember that antitheatrical tracts are pathological. They share assumptions with the culture as a whole, but their conclusions are eccentric. Stephen Greenblatt, in a brilliant essay, relates the development of the transvestite stage precisely to the cultural tropes of the body as they are anatomized in the medical and gynecological theories of the age, and he concludes that "a conception of gender that is teleologically male and insists upon a verifiable sign to confirm nature's final cause finds its supreme literary expression in a transvestite theatre."[11] This is an exciting and attractive thesis, but the problem with it is that the medical theorists are for the most part French and Italian, and France and Italy did not develop transvestite theatres. Why did only the English public theatre resist the introduction of women on the stage? As I have indicated, any attempt to answer this question by simply producing an explanation, whether social, religious or political, will only close off the ramifications of the question. But the context within which the issue can be understood must have to do with culture-specific attitudes toward women, and toward sexuality, and I want therefore now to consider its specifically sexual implications.

Despite the anxiety expressed in the antitheatrical literature, despite the institutionalization of marriage and patriarchy, English Renaissance culture, to judge from the surviving evidence, did not

35

display a morbid fear of homoeroticism as such; the love of men for other men was both a fact of life and an essential element of the patronage system. As Alan Bray demonstrates, the rhetoric of male friendship is precisely that of passionate, even overtly sexual love – the line between the homosocial and the sodomitical was a firm but exceedingly fine one, and lay in the most profound sense in the eye of the beholder.[12] Anxiety about the fidelity of women, on the other hand, does seem to have been strikingly prevalent; this is clear from nonliterary sources. Katharine Maus cites studies of sixteenth-century ecclesiastical courts in Essex and York which reveal that most of the defamation suits were prompted by three insulting terms: cuckold, whore and whoremaster.[13] The fear of losing control of women's chastity, a very valuable possession that guaranteed the legitimacy of one's heirs, and especially valuable for fathers as a piece of disposable property, is a logical consequence of a patriarchal structure – as the figure of Prospero, for example, with his compulsive fears about preserving his marriageable daughter's virginity, makes clear. One would have to have parallel statistics from Spain, France and Italy to know how much explanatory value the defamation records have; certainly cuckoldry seems to have been very much on the Italian mind in the Renaissance too. But these figures help to indicate the extent to which theatre served as a means of managing specifically sexual anxieties: Maus notes that the incidence of cuckoldry plots seems to be much higher in the drama than in the other imaginative genres of the period.

As far as paternal prerogatives were concerned, there were sufficient ambiguities within the English system to justify the anxieties of a father who assumed his rights over the disposition of his child to be absolute. Thus Egeus, in *A Midsummer Night's Dream*, has the law fully on his side in his insistence on his daughter's marriage to a man she does not love; nevertheless, by the end of the play Egeus has been overruled by the authority of the Duke, and Hermia is enabled to marry the man of her choice despite the law –

and Athenian law, as Shakespeare presents it, was even more stringent than Elizabethan law. English fathers were legally entitled to arrange their daughters' marriages as they saw fit, and of course had control of all property that accompanied the daughter; but until 1604 the legal age of consent was twelve for women (fourteen for men), which meant that daughters over the age of twelve were also legally entitled to arrange their own marriages. They might make themselves paupers by doing so, but they could not be stopped.[14] The horror stories of enforced marriages – there are many in the period – relate primarily to upper-class matches, where political alliances and large sums of money were at stake. In such cases, what the age of consent meant in practice was merely that a woman could not be forced to consent to a marriage arranged for her before she reached the age of twelve.

Middle- and lower-class arrangements, however, would have been much less constrained, as there was much less at stake. Indeed, middle-class London was a place of unusual liberty for women, and this certainly bears on both the popularity of the London theatre with women, and their relative freedom to enjoy it: the professional theatre drew much of its support from London's mercantile and artisan classes. It also probably accounts for the proliferation of plays about both love matches and cuckoldry, the two sides of the notion of liberty for women. That liberating theatrical freedom, however, could also be viewed as dangerous and anarchic, and the source of the danger was, as we have seen, assumed to be specifically sexual.

Public theatre is regularly associated, moreover, not only with loose women but with homosexual prostitution; the latter charge is found not only in Puritan polemicists but in the playwrights themselves. Yet the attitude implied in the charge tends to be, surprisingly, liberal and permissive. In Middleton's *Father Hubburd's Tales*, a budding London rake is advised "to call in at the Blackfriars, where he should see a nest of boys able to ravish a man."[15] In Jonson's *Poetaster*, Ovid's father, learning that Ovid has become a playwright,

37

and fearing that he will go on to become an actor, says, "What, shall I have my son a stager now, an ingle for players . . .?" (1.2.15–16). An ingle is a catamite; Alan Bray cites this and several other examples to show that the association was a common one;[16] but the theatres were not therefore avoided by decent folk or closed. The crime of sodomy is inveighed against repeatedly and energetically in legal and theological contexts; but, as Bray and Bruce Smith demonstrate, it was scarcely ever prosecuted.[17] When cases of homosexual behavior reach the courts, they are dealt with on the whole with surprising moderation – admonitions, exhortations to abstain. In fact, again, women are felt to pose the more serious problem: heterosexual fornication was much more energetically prosecuted. Magistrates took an interest in such cases because they resulted in illegitimate births, which increased the poor rolls, whereas, unless the activity involved coercion or malfeasance, there was rarely anything in homosexuality worth bothering about.[18]

In one extraordinary case discussed by Bray, a laborer named Meredith Davy was brought before the magistrate on what certainly could have been a charge of sodomy. Davy slept in the same bed with a twelve-year-old apprentice, and a third man slept in the same room. On a number of occasions the third man heard activity in the other bed, and heard the boy protest and cry out in pain. It took about a month for the witness to realize what was happening, and he finally reported it to the mistress of the house, who referred the case to the magistrate. The defendant appeared baffled by the charge, and clearly had no conception that what he was doing was related to the abominable crime of sodomy. This, surprisingly, seemed sufficient mitigation to the magistrate, and to the household as a whole; Davy was sent home with an admonishment to leave the boy alone, "since which time," the court report concludes, "he hath lain quietly with him."[19] The two, that is, were allowed to continue to sleep together; and of course it is conceivable that things quieted down not because Davy stopped making advances but because the boy stopped objecting – it was not, after all, the boy who made the complaint.

Bray argues that such a story does not testify to any remarkable tolerance on the part of the English, but rather to a selective blindness: sodomy was something that, despite a number of explicit charges and well-known prosecutions – the cases of Nicholas Udall, Francis Bacon, the Castlehaven scandal – the English associate on the whole only with foreigners, not with themselves. Travelers observing it in the relatively tolerant climates of Italy, Turkey, North Africa and Russia use it as an index to the viciousness of Roman Catholic, Muslim or barbaric societies.[20] And yet when, at the opening of *Epicoene*, Clerimont is shown with a page boy who is described as "his ingle," the fact serves as nothing more than one of a number of indications of the easy and pleasant life of a London playboy.[21] Similarly, in *The Alchemist*, Face persuades the doubting Kastril of Subtle's powers by citing the case of an all but bankrupt commander who has, through the alchemist's art, been enabled to

> Arrive at competent means, to keep himself,
> His punk, and naked boy, in excellent fashion,
> And be admired for't.   (3.4.80–2)

Marston introduces a little sodomitical joke into the exchange between the actors Sly and Sinklo in the introduction to *The Malcontent*:

SLY. Oh, cousin, come, you shall sit between my legs here.
SINKLO. No, indeed, cousin: the audience will then take me for a
     viol-de-gamba, and think that you play upon me.
SLY. Nay, rather that I work upon you, coz. (23–31)

"Work upon" means "have intercourse with," as Iago tells Desdemona and Emilia, "You rise to play, and go to bed to work."[22] This bit of overtly homoerotic titillation was obviously not expected to empty the theatre, though it is certainly relevant to Elizabethan assumptions about the sexual habits of actors. Charges of sodomy always occur in relation to other kinds of subversion; the activity has little independent existence in the Renaissance mind, just as there is not yet a separate category of the homosexual. It becomes visible in Elizabethan society only when it intersects with some other behavior that is recognized as dangerous and anti-social; it is invariably an aspect of atheism, Papistry, sedition, witchcraft, malfeasance – the conjunction is epitomised in John Aubrey's startlingly casual identification of Bacon as a pederast: "He was a παιδεραστής. His Ganimeds and Favourites tooke Bribes; but his Lordship alwayes gave Judgement *secundum aequum et bonum* [according to what was just and good]."[23] The reassurance is designed to counteract the logical inference that Bacon's sodomitical interests must have vitiated his judicial integrity; but it cannot be irrelevant that Bacon was impeached on charges of bribery and corrupt dealings. This is something Aubrey suppresses, though it is precisely the accusation he levels against the Ganymedes and Favorites.

The specifically irreligious character of sodomy is emphasized by Justice Coke, whose citations continually group it with heresy and sorcery. Paul Seaver records the account of a Puritan artisan,

that he had just heard of a group of married men in Southwark who had "lived in the sin of buggery and were sworn brothers to it" some seven years, committing this sin on Sabbath mornings at "sermon time."[24]

The artisan cites this as one of a number of London sins in punishment for which God sent a fire in 1633 that destroyed London Bridge, the City's connection to Southwark. What is striking here is that sodomy alone is felt to be insufficiently reprehensible; it is presented in addition as an affront to marriage, the sabbath, the church and the minister at his sermon. The catch-all quality of the act is clear from Henry Peacham's *Ganymede* emblem in *Minerva Britanna* (1612), in which the unfortunate youth is associated not only with sodomy, but with incest, witchcraft, murder and counterfeiting as well.[25] In the same way, the Puritan charge that theatre promotes homosexuality appears because to the Puritan mind theatre is felt to be dangerous, not the other way round; sodomy becomes the visible sign of its subversiveness.

King James's public and overtly physical displays of affection for young men are frequently remarked in the period; they are considered to be in bad taste (as are the king's manners generally), but not even the most rabid Puritan connects them with the abominable crime against nature.[26] And yet the Jacobean court, at least from the perspective of Charles I's Whitehall, was felt to be especially hospitable to homosexuality. Lucy Hutchinson, whose husband was a Roundhead colonel, saw in this a significant element in the transition from Jacobean to Caroline:

> The face of the court was much changed in the change of the king, for King Charles was temperate, chaste and serious; so that the fools and bawds, mimics and catamites of the former court grew out of fashion; and the nobility and courtiers, who did not quite abandon their debaucheries, yet so reverenced the king as to retire into corners to practise them.[27]

The disapproval of this Puritan woman discussing the debaucheries of catamites is colored by neither anxiety nor outrage. Tastes, she merely observes, change. Here, for comparison, is a passage from a letter written to Buckingham by King James:

> I cannot content myself without sending you this present, praying God that I may have a joyful and comfortable meeting with you and that we may make at this Christmas a new marriage ever to be kept hereafter; for, God so love me, as I desire only to live in the world for your sake, and that I had rather live banished in any part of the earth with you than live a sorrowful widow's life without you. And so God bless you, my sweet child and wife, and grant that ye may ever be a comfort to your dear dad and husband. James R.[28]

The metamorphic quality James adopts in this rhetoric is notable; he proposes marriage to Buckingham, and then imagines himself in succession as widow, father and husband, and Buckingham as his child and wife. The interchangeability of gender (and of the gender, moreover, of both parties) is here an essential element of the language of eros. This is the other side of the fear that love effeminates.

Nor is there anything inappropriate or even unusual in such linguistic profligacy: I have already cited Alan Bray's observation that the rhetoric of patronage, gratitude and male friendship in the period is precisely the language of love, rendering all such relationships literally ambiguous. He goes on to argue that the relationships implied are therefore not to be read as homosexual in the modern sense, that is, that they do not imply a sexual relationship; but though this is doubtless true as far as it goes, Jonathan Goldberg points out that it was precisely the world of public discourse that was the space of homoerotic relationships.[29] The love between men was open and public, in this case an index to the king's lavish beneficence towards Buckingham and to the favorite's enviable place in the royal favor. How far beyond beneficence and gratitude that love went is imponderable, and there is nothing in the language of love that will reveal it to us – it is a language that implies everything and nothing.

Though there are any number of passionate heterosexual relationships depicted in English Renaissance literature, it is also a commonplace to find a generalized misogyny in the work of the period, especially in its idealization of chaste and beautiful women who are also cold and untouchable. What is less often observed is that along with the varieties of conventional romance, romantic and even erotic homosexual relationships also figure in the literature of the period, in a context that is often, if not invariably, positive, and registers again, even when the underlying attitude is disapproving, surprisingly little anxiety about the matter. I am not talking here about what in modern terms would be called male bonding, where no explicit sexual component is acknowledged; though there certainly is a good deal of that in Renaissance literature. I am talking about explicitly sexual relationships. Consider the fact that Rosalind disguised as a boy can play a wooing scene with another man under the name Ganymede. The peculiar and pathological element in this is not that Orlando is therefore involved in playing a love scene with a man. It is that so few critics (and none cited in the variorum) have ever remarked that the model for it must be a homosexual flirtation; the name Ganymede cannot be used in the Renaissance without this connotation. But there is no indication whatever that Shakespeare is doing something sexually daring there, skating on thin ice. Counterexamples in which homoerotic behavior leads to disaster are exceedingly rare. The only clear-cut theatrical one is in Marlowe's *Edward II* (and in the career of Marlowe generally), and I shall return to this; but first I want to cite a number of other instances.

The young shepherd Colin in *The Shepherd's Calendar* rejects the advances of the older shepherd Hobbinol, "Albe my love he seek with daily suit: / His clownish gifts and curtsies I disdain." Colin instead pursues the unresponsive Rosalind.[30] Hobbinol's flirtation is presented simply as part of the poet–shepherd's experience; but since Colin is identified in the book as Spenser, and Hobbinol as Gabriel Harvey, the allusion seems to have a specific application as well, to be saying something about the relationship between Spenser and Harvey. Spenser clearly does not consider this libelous, and judging from their continued association, neither did Harvey; but it makes the volume's editor E. K. nervous, and in glossing the passage he duly cites the relevant classical precedents of Socrates and Alcibiades. These lead him to the conclusion that "paederistike [is] much to be preferred before gynerastike, that is the love which enflameth men with lust toward womankind." He adds only at this point that he is not thereby condoning (or, presumably, implying that Harvey is guilty of) the "execrable and horrible sins of forbidden and unlawful fleshliness" celebrated by Lucian and Pietro Aretino.[31]

43

The strategy here is significant, and to modern eyes puzzling. In order to disarm the allusion, E. K. need only have cited Virgil's second eclogue, which he has already recognized as one of Spenser's principal sources: here the poet imitateth Virgil. But instead he gives an argument from classical authority in defence of pederasty and against heterosexual love. This is entirely unnecessary as a strategy on Spenser's behalf, since Colin has rejected Hobbinol in favor of Rosalind. Nevertheless, E. K. wants to insist on the privileged status of homosexuality, not as an aspect of poetry, but of the highest moral philosophy – Socrates authorized it. To do this it is only necessary to deflect the prohibited aspects of homosexual behavior onto women on the one hand, and Italians on the other. It is important to observe that despite Colin's interest in Rosalind, there is no argument here in favor of the love of women, and that homosexual love is defined in opposition to heterosexuality, which is equated with lust.[32]

Marlowe, in *Hero and Leander*, expresses a good deal more enthusiasm for the physical side of homoeroticism. He also, like the antitheatrical polemicists, assumes both the irresistible force of sexual desire and the power of attractive youths to elicit it specifically from male observers, though this is a source of excitement rather than panic. When Leander is first described, he is praised primarily for his erotic effect on men. Cynthia, apparently alone among women, "wished his arms might be her sphere"; whereas Leander's hair

> Would have allured the venturous youth of Greece
> To hazard more than for the Golden Fleece;   (57–8)

he could have replaced Ganymede as Jove's cupbearer; if Hippolytus had seen Leander, he would have abandoned his chastity and fallen in love with him; the rudest peasant and the barbarous Thracian soldier sought his favor. After this, it is not surprising that he attracts the attentions of Neptune, who mistakes him for Ganymede, and is described in an extraordinarily explicit passage making passes

44

at Leander as he swims naked to Sestos. The episode is notable for the total lack of anxiety it projects. It is passionate, comic, and enthusiastic.

In *Troilus and Cressida*, Patroclus urges Achilles to return to the battlefield:

> To this effect, Achilles, have I moved you.
> A woman impudent and mannish grown
> Is not more loathed than an effeminate man
> In time of action. I stand condemned for this.
> They think my little stomach to the war
> And your great love to me restrains you thus.
> Sweet, rouse yourself; and the weak wanton Cupid
> Shall from your neck unloose his amorous fold
> And, like a dew-drop from the lion's mane,
> Be shook to air. (3.3.216–25)

The language is the language of love, but the terms might have been borrowed from any polemicist; and Thersites comes straight out with it: there is nothing Platonic about the relationship between the two heroes – Patroclus is "Achilles' male varlet . . . his masculine whore" (5.1.14–16). Thersites is not the most reliable of witnesses, but the play makes no attempt to represent Achilles and Patroclus as innocent of the abominable crime. Achilles is unmanned, however, by love itself, not by its object, which turns out at the crucial moment to be female as well as male. He is also in love with Priam's daughter Polyxena, and it is the love of women that finally proves antithetical to the claims of martial heroism:

> My sweet Patroclus, I am thwarted quite
> From my great purpose in tomorrow's battle.
> Here is a letter from Queen Hecuba,
> A token from her daughter, my fair love,
> Both taxing me and gaging me to keep
> An oath that I have sworn. I will not break it.

Fall Greeks, fail fame, honor or go or stay,
My major vow lies here; this I'll obey.   (5.1.36–43)

To my knowledge the only dramatic instance of a homoerotic
relationship being presented in the terms in which the culture
formally conceived it – as antisocial, seditious, ultimately disastrous –
is in Marlowe's *Edward II*. It would certainly be possible to account
for its perspective, if not for its uniqueness, by viewing it in the
context of Eve Sedgwick's thesis about Renaissance homosexuality:
that it was not viewed as threatening because it was not defined in
opposition to, or as an impediment to, heterosexuality and
marriage.[33] Edward's love for Gaveston therefore is destructive
because it *is* presented as antiheterosexual; it renders him an unfit
husband, as his passion renders him an unfit king. I am unhappy with
this explanation not because there is anything wrong with it, but
because it is too straightforward to account for what seems to me a
very devious and genuinely subversive play. Both politically and
morally, the power-hungry nobles and the queen's adultery with
Mortimer are as destabilizing as anything in Edward's relationship
with his favorite. (Indeed, the title page declares the play a double
tragedy, concerned with both "the troublesome reign and
lamentable death of Edward II" and "the tragical fall of proud
Mortimer.") The real complaint against Gaveston has to do not with
his sexuality, but with the fact that he is being given preferments
over other powerful and ambitious courtiers, even to the extent of
being given Edward's niece in marriage – marriage here is fully
complicit with homoeroticism, and the path to success, not only for
Gaveston, is through the king's love. Marlowe makes Gaveston an
upstart, raised to the nobility by the king's infatuation with him, and
the social inappropriateness of the love is a central element in the
presentation of Edward as a sodomite.[34] The social issue is clearly
important to Marlowe, since the historical Gaveston was in fact a
gentleman, the son of a Gascon knight who had served Edward I

with distinction; the young Gaveston was raised at court as the young Edward's foster brother and playmate – raised, that is, to be his favorite. The Elizabethan chroniclers are eloquent, even vehement, about the evil influence Gaveston had over the king, leading him into extravagance and dissolute pleasures, even persuading him to commit adultery; but (though John Speed expresses distaste for his "effeminate" subject) none of this produces a charge of sodomy – the charge is Marlowe's.

And in important respects ours: modern performances always, and critics nearly always, construe the murder scene as an anal rape with a hot spit or poker. But this is "correcting" Marlowe by reference to Holinshed: at the beginning of the murder scene, Lightborne directs that a red-hot spit be prepared, and asks also for a table and a feather bed; these are the murder weapons authorized by history, though Holinshed makes the table and the feather bed alternatives, observing that some of his sources mention one, some the other. In the event, however, Lightborne ignores Holinshed and sends his accomplice Matrevis only for the table. Here is the passage:

KING EDWARD. I am too weak and feeble to resist.
    Assist me, sweet God, and receive my soul.
LIGHTBORNE. Run for the table.
KING EDWARD. O spare me, or dispatch me in a trice.
LIGHTBORNE. So lay the table down and stamp on it,
    But not too hard, lest that you bruise his body.
MATREVIS. I fear me that this cry will raise the town.
    And therefore let us take horse and away. (5.5.107–14)

Edward is pressed to death; directors who want the spit to be used have to send Lightborne off stage to fetch it himself – tables are two-handed engines. It might be worth considering why, for modern commentators, that unused spit is so irresistible – Bruce Smith, for example, insists that "though the speeches and stage directions mention nothing about this spit while Edward is being crushed . . .

47

the cry he lets out leaves little doubt that Lightborne puts the spit to just the use specified in Holinshed's *Chronicles,*"[35] as if being crushed to death were not sufficient motivation for crying out. David H. Thurn, in an otherwise exceedingly perceptive reading, does not even notice the table, but kills the king "with the brutal thrust of a 'red-hot' poker," and Gregory Bredbeck's excellent chapter on the play unintentionally provides an epitome of modern revisionism: "The murder of Edward by raping him with a red-hot poker – quite literally branding him with sodomy – can be seen as an attempt to 'write' onto him the homoeroticism constantly ascribed to him."[36] It can indeed: we want the murder to be precisely what Marlowe refuses to make it, a condign punishment, the mirror of Edward's unspeakable vice.

For Marlowe to translate the whole range of power politics into sodomy certainly says something about his interests and that of Elizabethan audiences, but it also has to be added that it was probably safer to represent the power structure in that way than it would have been to play it, so to speak, straight. Had Richard II been presented as a sodomite, would the authorities have found it necessary to censor the deposition scene? Maybe Edward's sexuality is a way of protecting the play, a way of keeping what it says about power intact. This is the work of Marlowe the government spy, at once an agent of the establishment and deeply subversive. And if we look forward, Edward's relation to Gaveston provides so clear a mirror of King James's behavior toward Carr, Buckingham, and the other favorites that it is startling to find the play was reissued in 1612 and again in 1622, and was performed publicly in that year. In fact, in 1621, in an inflammatory parliamentary speech, Sir Henry Yelverton had made the analogy between James's treatment of Buckingham and Edward's of his favorites explicit – the particular favorite cited was not Gaveston but his successor Hugh Spencer, but the point was not lost on James and Buckingham. James demanded a retraction on the grounds that the comparison represented him as a weak king, and Yelverton was forced to apologize and heavily fined.[37] Had it been possible for a Jacobean audience to acknowledge sodomy as an English vice, the play, and the allusion, would certainly have been treasonable.

In the examples we have considered, the love of men for men in this culture appears less threatening than the love of men for women: it had fewer consequences, it was easier to de-sexualize, it figured and reinforced the patronage system. But beneath these practical considerations was a deep layer of anxiety. The reason always given for the prohibition of women from the stage was that their chastity would thereby be compromised, which is understood to mean that they would become whores. The problem here is obviously not with theatre but with women, on whom the culture projects a natural tendency towards promiscuity of all kinds, and for which theatre is being seen as a release mechanism. Behind the outrage of public modesty is a real fear of women's sexuality, and more specifically, of its power to evoke men's sexuality; this is the fear expressed in Polixenes' Edenic fantasy about life before puberty, and in Leontes' paranoid retreat from his wife. It is a fear that denies the claims of the gynecology of inverted, incomplete masculinity, a fear grounded in a recognition not of sameness but of difference, and of the desire that proceeds from it. This desire is dangerous because it is not subject to rational control, which is a way of saying that it is not subject to any other kind of authority either – what from one perspective was slavery to passion, from another was a declaration of freedom; and this of course bears on the question of what Renaissance women found attractive about a theatre we find misogynistic.

Shakespearean drama often confronts these anxieties; comedy looks for ways to control them, they constitute a subject for tragedy. Othello's and Iago's assumptions about Desdemona, and about women generally, include all the familiar claims of Renaissance treatises on women and the dangers of the stage; they are false in this case, but Desdemona's chastity does not save her or Othello from a tragic outcome. Moreover, critics with patriarchal leanings might argue, and have on occasion done so, that the real source of the tragedies of Desdemona and Juliet is their refusal to obey their fathers, the declaration of freedom implicit in their insistence on choosing their own husbands. In one respect, these plays exemplify a perfectly standard patriarchalist and anti-feminist line, and though Elizabethan audiences would certainly have responded to their tragic force, it is doubtful that any Elizabethan spectator would have found them subversive.

Stephen Greenblatt has related the transvestitism of figures like Portia, Rosalind and Viola to the teleology of masculinity implied by the medical and gynecological theories cited earlier. Such figures, in this reading, "pass through the state of being men in order to become women. Shakespearean women are in this sense the projected mirror images of masculine self-differentiation."[38] But even this clearly has its anxieties: Shakespeare shows on occasion an unwillingness to allow them to return to being women. In an ending that has been almost totally ignored, if not positively misrepresented by the critical tradition, Viola announces in the final moments of *Twelfth Night* that she cannot become a woman and the wife of Orsino until her woman's clothes have been recovered – a dress borrowed from Olivia or a new one purchased for the occasion apparently are not options – and that this will require the release of the sea captain who alone can find them, which in turn will necessitate the mollification of the enraged Malvolio, who has had the sea captain incarcerated: this all materializes out of nowhere in the last three minutes of the play, and Malvolio at the play's end offers no assistance but runs from the stage shouting "I'll be revenged on the whole pack of you." For Viola to become a woman requires, in short, a whole new play with Malvolio at its center.[39] Rosalind, speaking the epilogue to *As You Like It*, reminds us that she is a boy, and that the drama has not represented an erotic and heterosexual reality at all: "If I were a woman, I would kiss as many of you as have beards that pleased me." This is the only place in Shakespeare where the heroine undoes her gender in this way (though Cleopatra at one moment approaches it). And yet Rosalind is surely among the most attractive and successful of Shakespeare's women: it must be to the point that Shakespeare does not want to leave her intact. I think it is also to the point that *Twelfth Night* includes the only overtly homosexual couple in Shakespeare except for Achilles and Patroclus.[40] What the presence of Antonio and Sebastian acknowledges, in a play that has at its center a man wooing a man, is that men *do* fall in love with other men. "You are betrothed," Sebastian tells Olivia, "both to a maid and man," recalling the master–mistress of Shakespeare's passion in the Sonnets. The same point is made by giving Rosalind the name Ganymede.

Jonathan Goldberg rejects, with some indignation, the notion that boys are seen as substitutes for women in this culture, and that Renaissance homoeroticism is therefore a version of heterosexuality, if only a safer one. In a passionate and subtle argument, he locates the erotics of masculine love not within the secret conclaves of Puritan polemicists, but in the most public areas of Renaissance life – this is the other side of the terrifying indefiniteness of sodomy to the Renaissance mind. This is certainly correct, a convincing and even liberating argument; but it is blinkered insofar as it underestimates the importance of the analogy between boys and women in the culture. This hardly needs to be demonstrated: Rosalind reminds Orlando that in matters of love the two are all but identical – "boys and women are for the most part cattle of this color" (1.2.388–9). Handsome boys were praised in Renaissance England by saying that they looked like women – "A woman's face, by Nature's own hand painted / Hast thou, the master–mistress of my passion." Even Gaveston, Goldberg's prime example of the masculine love object in the period, entertains his beloved Edward with lascivious dances performed by "a lovely boy in Dian's shape"; the cross-dressing is clearly not irrelevant to the lasciviousness. So it cannot be the case that the love of boys has *nothing* to do with the love of women in this culture. That this is not all there is to say about Renaissance homoeroticism is undeniable; the question is what the two have to do with each other: what do boys and women have in common that distinguishes both from men, and renders both objects of desire for men?

4

Call me Ganymede

L et us consider two unusual, indeed unique, Shakespearean erotic substitutions that have been all but ignored by editors and critics. These are strikingly self-reflexive moments in which Shakespeare makes the practice of his theatre, the substitution of boys for women, into the subject of his drama; but they are moments that have been, in effect, rendered invisible.

At the opening of *Twelfth Night*, Viola, shipwrecked, orphaned, and believing that she has seen her twin brother Sebastian drowned, proposes attaching herself to the similarly orphaned Olivia, who is also in mourning for her dead brother. When told that this is impossible, that Olivia "will admit no kind of suit," Viola conceives a much more complex scheme. She says she will present herself to the Duke Orsino, Olivia's unrequited suitor, as "an eunuch," and "sing, / And speak to him in many sorts of music." She then dresses herself in male clothing, calls herself Cesario, and enters Orsino's service, acting as his page, confidant and the agent of his love.

The choice of the name Cesario for Viola as eunuch has gone unremarked, but it seems to me to have a good deal of resonance. Cesario is the Italian form of the Latin *Caesarius*, "belonging to Caesar" (and hence untouchable – in Wyatt's words, "*Noli me tangere, for Caesar's I am*"[1]), but we can also find in it what etymologists from Varro onward found in the name Caesar itself, the past participle of *caedo*, *caesus*, "cut," alluding in Caesar's case to his Caesarian birth. Cesario's own claim of castration goes no further than this; we hear no more about it (though the play has some fun with the word "cut"), and Viola does not perform as a singer or musician anywhere in the action. Her silence, to be sure, may be a function of the textual history of the play – that is, there may once have been a version of *Twelfth Night* in which Viola *was* a musician, the true love "that can sing both high and low." But textual histories are nevertheless histories, and revisions, elisions, suppressions, accretions are essential elements of drama by its very nature. The text we have, moreover, is certainly more real than any text we might invent to account for a putative lacuna.

The question, then, is not how this moment functions dramatically, since in any practical sense it does not function at all, but, precisely because of its discreteness and uniqueness, what cultural implications it has. That single moment when Viola conceives herself as a eunuch has received very little editorial attention. The word "eunuch" is always glossed as if it were simply a term for a male treble voice, with no underlying history of surgical procedures. This, however, is an editorial fantasy; there is no such usage recorded in English. As with the later term "castrato," "eunuch" only meant "singer" if the singer was a eunuch. We ought therefore to confront the implications of Viola's conceiving herself as not simply a youth in disguise, but as surgically neutered in addition. She seems to be proposing a sexlessness that is an aspect of her mourning, that will effectively remove her, as Olivia has removed herself, from the world of love and wooing.

This in itself, however, is problematical: as Shakespeare's eunuch Mardian complains, the surgery incapacitates only sexual performance; the desire remains as intense as ever – "Yet have I fierce affections, and think / What Venus did with Mars."[2] If Mardian is to be our guide, Viola has with a single word created for herself a character in whom frustrated sexual desire is of the essence – created, in fact, the role she performs in the play. But there is a peculiar overtone as well: being a eunuch, a sexually incapacitated male, is conceived as an equivalent, or an alternative, to being a woman. This fantasy is a very old one: Chaucer, expressing his doubts about the Pardoner's sexuality, describes him as "a geldying or a mare."[3] Cleopatra makes the same point even more explicitly, inviting Mardian to play billiards with her: "As well a woman with an eunuch played / As with a woman."[4] What is missing in their play is what billiards is played with, a rod and balls – the essential element in sexuality is, in this formulation, male potency. The moment acts out a classic Freudian fantasy, whereby gender difference is a function of castration. *Twelfth Night* makes the fantasy all but explicit in its puns on "cut" and "cunt." If a eunuch is an alternative to a woman, and either is the opposite of a man, then the assumptions behind Viola's disguise desexualize women too.

Or do they? A brief look at the history of castrati complicates the question. The eunuch–singers in Shakespeare's time were the most famous choirboys of the Roman Catholic church, used first in Spain from the early sixteenth century, and subsequently, most notoriously, in the Vatican. The paternal decision to castrate a son to make him eligible for choir school sounds like a particularly radical and invasive instance of patriarchal authority in action, but we should consider whether it is in fact much more radical than the absolute right exercised by fathers in arranging their children's marriages. In a Renaissance Catholic society, good arguments could be produced in favor of castrating your son – the same good arguments as those involved in deciding that he was going to have a career as a priest or a monk, or in sending your daughter into a convent. Such decisions guaranteed the child a good and, in the case of castrati, often lucrative career; and celibacy, if you were serious about your religion, was a virtue.[5] Castration had the disadvantage of being irreversible (marriage was usually irreversible too), but the advantages, in terms of income and security, were correspondingly large. This all sounds appalling to us, but the practice continued through the eighteenth century. The Vatican castrati quickly started playing secular roles as well as religious ones: like the boys on the

English stage, they played the romantic women's parts in entertainments for the exclusively male society of the Catholic hierarchy. In this respect the boys were not at all desexualized; on the contrary, they enabled the introduction of overt sexuality, simultaneously heterosexual and homosexual, into the world of ecclesiastical celibacy.

Viola as eunuch, then, both closes down options for herself and implies a world of possibilities for others – possibilities that were, to a post-Reformation Protestant society, particularly (perhaps temptingly) illicit. The possibilities are conceived precisely in terms of sexual alternatives and equivalents of either-and-both; as Viola says to the uncomprehending Orsino, "I am all the daughters of my father's house, / And all the brothers too," and as her twin Sebastian, fresh from his adoring Antonio, says to Olivia, "You are betrothed both to a maid and man." This double-gendered figure realizes Shakespeare's master–mistress of Sonnet 20, the young man who is such a powerfully desirable alternative to a woman: better looking, less deceitful, more faithful; who has all the advantages of women with no disadvantages. Except, as the poem ends, one: the fact that he is "pricked out"; but it is not really clear that this constitutes a disadvantage. Sex, as all the sonnets in this sequence imply, is dangerous and destabilizing when you do it with women; but love is what you do with men – nor is it clear that the love between men, even in Sonnet 20, is necessarily nonsexual. The poem certainly denies that the speaker and his love are sleeping together; but if it is really true that men do not go to bed with other men because they have pricks, then the need for the denial is more significant than the denial itself. Whatever the speaker is doing with the master–mistress of his passion, Shakespeare's disclaimer insists on the reality of sex between men. Indeed, behind the final couplet,

> since [nature] pricked thee out for women's pleasure,
> Mine be thy love, and thy love's use their treasure,

Stephen Booth finds a Martial epigram that says, "Nature has divided the male: one part is made for girls, one for men"[6] – boys have something for everyone. Moreover, as both Randall McLeod and Peter Stallybrass have remarked to me, in an unmodernized text, the couplet does in fact allow for an explicitly sexual relationship between the poet and the young man. Here are the lines as they appeared in 1609, with only the typography modernized:

> But since she prickt thee out for womens pleasure,
> Mine be thy love and thy loves use their treasure.

In this reading, "But" signals a reversal of the argument, and means "on the other hand": the "womens pleasure" the youth is "pricked out for" (i.e. selected for: see *OED s.* prick III.15) is not the pleasure he gives women but his ability to take pleasure as women do; "loves" in the last line is then not a possessive but a plural, and "use" is a verb – the line without its modern apostrophe need not be a renunciation at all: "let my love be yours, and let your loves make use of their treasure."[7] If we look at *Twelfth Night* in this context, Orsino and Olivia have fallen in love with the same young man, Cesario; only the costume, the chosen role, distinguishes Cesario from Viola and Viola from the Sebastian who is effortlessly substituted for her in Olivia's affections. The gender of these figures is mutable, constructed, a matter of choice.[8]

If Viola the eunuch equivocates her sexuality, Rosalind as Ganymede in *As You Like It* makes the equation between women and boys not only explicit, but explicitly sexual. And here the idea of the boy displacing the woman appears in its most potentially threatening form, the catamite for whom Jove himself abandons his marriage bed. Why is this inescapable allusion a part of Orlando's and Rosalind's wooing? Why do the sexual dynamics of Orlando's love include not simply a boy, but the one boy capable of incapacitating his marriage? And why do the sexual dynamics of Rosalind's love involve her in not merely disguising herself as the dangerous alternative, but in maintaining her disguise as Ganymede even after she knows Orlando loves her as Rosalind? "Alas the day," she says to Celia in the middle of act 3, when the play is less than half over, "what shall I do with my doublet and hose?" – what is the point of my male clothing now? It is a real question, one that the play is willing to confront, but that editors have been almost without exception shy of.

I observed earlier that English Renaissance culture does not appear to have had a morbid fear of male homoerotic behavior, and I cited a number of instances where the love of men for boys (homosexuality is generally, though not exclusively, conceived to be pederastic in the period) is assumed to be inherently preferable to the love of men for women. The abominable crime of sodomy was fervently condemned throughout the age, but the legal definition of sodomy was in fact exceedingly narrow. According to the Lord Chief Justice Sir Edward Coke, the sex had to be nonconsensual – that is, it had to be a rape; the prosecution had to be able to prove that there had been both anal penetration and an ejaculation ("*emissio seminis*" alone, Coke observes, "maketh it not buggery"); and in actual practice, the courts required a witness – and there were strict rules about who could serve as a witness in such cases. The laws of Renaissance England as elucidated by Justice Coke said nothing about sex between consenting male partners, about sex between men other than anal sex, about homosexual activity of any kind performed in private: none of these legally constituted sodomy.[9]

The legal situation does not at all coincide with popular attitudes, of course, in which the term sodomy covered a multitude of horrendous sins, not all of them by any means involving homosexuality; but precisely for this reason it is to the point that sodomy was legally construed in such a way that it could hardly ever be prosecuted. Coke's definition was developed in Jacobean times (and the third part of the *Institutes*, in which the definition finally

58

appears, was not published until 1644), but though the statutory language relating to sodomy was always portentously vague ("the most horrible and detestable vice . . . to the high displeasure of almightie God," etc.[10]), and sounds like a license for indiscriminate prosecution, it is evident that Coke's analysis is firmly based on judicial precedent: Bruce Smith's study of the Assize courts in the Home Counties reveals a total of only six sodomy trials in the entire reign of Elizabeth; all involved the rape of a minor, and five of the six resulted in aquittals.[11] Legally, in effect, buggery was defined as pederastic rape: as Smith puts it, Coke "treats the forcible rape of an underaged boy as the only kind of [sodomitical] act in which the law takes an interest."[12] In the particular precedent Coke cites, a 1607 case of the rape of a sixteen-year-old youth, the victim's age too is significant: he was legally a minor; but the age of consent had been raised from fourteen to twenty-one only three years earlier. If the act had been committed in 1603, it is not clear that it would even have been considered criminal.

Sodomy, then, does not mean what we mean by homosexuality. As proliferating studies in the history of sexuality have shown, the binary division of sexual appetites into the normative heterosexual and the deviant homosexual is a very recent invention; neither homosexuality nor heterosexuality existed as categories for the Renaissance mind. Indeed, the very idea that sexual preferences constitute categories – that people can be identified according to what kinds of sex they enjoy – and moreover that such categories are exclusive ones – that an interest in men necessarily precludes or conflicts with an interest in women – is largely a piece of post-Enlightenment taxonomy.[13] Men in the period who preferred not to marry – like two of Shakespeare's Antonios – were eccentric, certainly, but they did not therefore constitute a special class, nor are they associated with the discourse of sodomy.

Indeed, overt imputations of sodomy in the drama rarely treat it as an exclusive taste, and are, as I have suggested, more often a subject for comedy than for moral outrage. In Fletcher's *The Honest Man's Fortune* (1613), a courtier named Laverdine is attracted to Veramour, a handsome page, because he looks like a woman, and woos him:

LAVERDINE. Thou art a pretty boy . . . I have not seen a youth that
hath pleased me better: I would thou couldst like me, so far as
to leave thy lady and wait on me! . . . Thy lodging –
VERAMOUR. Should be in a brothel.
LAVERDINE. No; but in mine arms.
VERAMOUR. That may be the circle of a bawdy-house, or worse.
LAVERDINE. I mean thou shalt lie with me.
VERAMOUR. Lie with you! I had rather lie with my lady's monkey:
'twas never good world since our French lords learned of the
Neapolitans to make their pages their bedfollows . . .[14]

The displacement of the desire onto the French and Italians is sufficient to render it comic. Veramour's response should establish him as both male and unseduceable, but Laverdine decides that Veramour's refusal can only indicate that he is in fact a woman. Veramour's defense against the vicissitudes of being a pretty boy is then to claim that he is, in truth, a woman in disguise; but this of course is just what Laverdine wants, and he at once proposes marriage. At the play's end Veramour appears in woman's dress and much is made of the difficulty of distinguishing boys and women; though here, unlike the end of *Twelfth Night*, clothes do not make the woman: it is observed that "a blind man by the hand / Could have discover'd the ring from the stone,"[15] both determined its quality and distinguished the vagina from testicles. Thus unmasked, Veramour announces his intention of going to the city to become an apprentice, and Laverdine is finally vanquished by the revelation that his beloved is really male; though given the obvious catholicity of a sexual taste that finds attractive boys indistinguishable from women, the logic of this resolution is not airtight. But the idea that being an apprentice is an alternative to being a woman is one that, as we shall see, has significant cultural implications.

The metamorphic quality of gender in such a scene is paradigmatic, and the paradigm remained unchanged until almost the end of the seventeenth century. We might compare it to a similar scene in Thomas Southerne's *Sir Anthony Love* (1690), in which the eponymous hero, actually a woman disguised as a youth, is propositioned by a lecherous, elderly French abbé: "We're very luckily alone, and shou'd make a good use of our time; no body will come to disturb us . . . I vow I'll teize you, and kiss you into good humour." Sir Anthony cuts short the proposal by revealing that he is a woman, and the abbé retires in confusion, begging her "to muzzle the scandal" – in its comic context, the scandal is less that he has been discovered making a pass at a man than that he has for once made a pass at a woman.[16] English satire had identified foreign Papist priests as sodomites since the Reformation, but in fact the implications of the flirtation are even less determinedly homoerotic than Fletcher's had been three-quarters of a century earlier. This youth, after all, unlike Veramour, is only pretending to be male; and the abbé is initially attracted to him not by his masculinity, but precisely by the femininity of his features, observing that "One might indeed mistake him, by his face."[17] In its conviction that the subtext of homoeroticism is really heterosexual, the scene might have been devised by a latter-day Rainoldes or Stubbes.

In Vanbrugh's *The Relapse* (1697), we can see that the paradigm has at last changed: homoeroticism is both unqualified and domesticated in the person of the lecherous Coupler – this is the first character I know of who would be recognizable as gay in the modern sense. A young man named Fashion is negotiating with Coupler, a professional matchmaker, for his aid in securing both a wife and his patrimony. Coupler immediately makes a pass at the young man:

61

COUPLER. . . . Ha, you young lascivious rogue, you! Let me put my
    hand in your bosom, sirrah.
FASHION. Stand off, old Sodom!

But when Coupler assures the youth that he can indeed help him,
here is the result:

FASHION. Sayest thou so, old Satan? Show me but that, and my
    soul is thine.
COUPLER. Pox o'thy soul, give me thy warm body, sirrah. I shall
    have a substantial title to't when I tell thee my project.
FASHION. Out with it then, dear dad, and take possession as soon
    as thou wilt.
COUPLER. Sayst thou so, my Hephestion? . . . [18]

The unabashed overtness and singlemindedness of Coupler's sexual
appetite, unmitigated by foreignness or Roman Catholicism, is in its
way even more striking than Fashion's easy aquiescence, and does
seem to be genuinely new – a significant step beyond the
freewheeling polymorphousness celebrated only two decades earlier
in Lord Rochester's *Sodom*, for example, or the equitable alternatives
proposed in "The Maim'd Debauchee" for the sexual enjoyment of a
handsome servant:

> Nor shall our Love-fits, Cloris, be forgot,
> When each the well-look'd Link-Boy, strove t'enjoy
> And the best Kiss, was the deciding Lot,
> Whether the Boy us'd you, or I the Boy. [19]

The line of descent from the view of sexuality implied in
Shakespeare's "master–mistress" sonnet to this is perfectly clear.
Vanbrugh marks a shift, though doubtless a less radical one in the
theatre than on the page, since Fashion was played in the original
production, as attractive young men often were on the Restoration
stage, by a woman. To use the terms homosexual and heterosexual to
describe the pre-Enlightenment situation, therefore, is anachronistic

and misleading. A much more direct way of putting the situation expressed in *As You Like It*, would be that eroticized boys appear to be a middle term between men and women, and far from precluding the love of women, they are represented as *enabling* figures, as a way of getting from men to women. But they also destabilize the categories, and question what it means to be a man or a woman.

Rosalind's doublet and hose therefore register the same cultural anxiety that is expressed in Galenic gynecology, and in the Elizabethan judicial practice relating to fornication. In a society that has an investment in seeing women as imperfect men, the danger points will be those at which women reveal that they have an independent essence, an existence that is not, in fact, under male control, a power and authority that either challenges male authority, or, more dangerously, that is not simply a version or parody of maleness, but is specifically female. In romance plots, this point is reached when the wooing starts, when the woman's separateness becomes essential, and her sexual nature has to be taken into account. This is the moment in *Twelfth Night* and *As You Like It* when Viola and Rosalind start to feel trapped by their disguises rather than protected by them. The Renaissance fantasy about women's sexuality is that it is voracious, uncontrollable, capable of enslaving and exhausting men – that it is, in short, male sexuality out of control: the great danger in women's sexuality is its power to evoke men's sexuality. In this context Rosalind's male disguise would be, in the deepest sense, for Orlando's benefit, not for Rosalind's; it would constitute a way around the dangers of the female libido. It is clear from Rosalind's epilogue, however, that the disguise is not only for Orlando's benefit, nor need it be so narrowly construed. In a moment unique in Shakespeare, the heroine directly addresses the men in the audience and undoes her gender: "If I were a woman, I would kiss as many of you as had beards that pleased me . . ." Even after the wooing has been successfully accomplished, the play insists that the wife is really a boy – and this too, of course, may be a way of offering Orlando (or any number of spectators of either sex) what he "really" wants.

The demystification, destabilizing, deconstruction of the Shakespearean text has increasingly become the business of criticism, and to read the plays through Renaissance documents, rather than through our own, refigures them, often radically. It can be argued that this is a historical claim only in a special sense, and that the plays are thereby being refigured not as Renaissance texts but as modern or postmodern ones; but in fact all claims about the past except the most narrowly archeological are historical in the same sense: they assume – often, to be sure, without acknowledging it – that we are involved in history as much as Shakespeare or Galen or archival documents. However responsible we undertake to be to our texts and their contexts, we can look only with our own eyes, and interpret only with our own minds, which have been formed by our own history. All historical claims, even the most tactful and unpoliticized, are ultimately concerned to make the past comprehensible, usable and relevant to our own interests – to make it, that is, present. Even for documentary historians (as even historians are beginning to be aware) the Renaissance changes with every generation.

I want to turn now to the practical reality behind Viola as eunuch and Rosalind as catamite, the position of boys in the Elizabethan theatre company, and their relation to the female roles they played and to the women in the audience. Standard theatrical history holds that the boys of the company were its apprentices, that they got their training playing women's roles and, when their voices changed, they progressed to playing adult males. But there are several problems with this version of the situation. To begin with, the boys *were* apprenticed, but not to the actors of the company, or at least, not in their capacity as actors: only members of guilds could have apprentices, and there was no actors' guild. The boys were apprenticed instead to those actors who happened to be guild members, of which there were a substantial number – in Shakespeare's company, for example, John Heminges was a grocer, Robert Armin and John Lowin were goldsmiths, and a number of other guilds were represented as well. The boys of the troupe were thus technically not apprentice actors but apprentice grocers, goldsmiths, drapers, shoemakers, joiners, and so forth, and when they completed their apprenticeships they were (or were entitled to be) full members of whatever guild they had been apprenticed in. A great deal has always been made of Ben Jonson's early training as a bricklayer, and in fact David Riggs has recently discovered that Jonson, despite his notorious distaste for the craft, renewed his membership in the bricklayers' guild in 1599, long after he became an actor (the receipt for his back dues – astonishingly – survives).[20] Riggs takes this to imply that Jonson was hedging his bets against the possibility of failure on the stage. On the contrary, it indicates to me his definitive incorporation into Henslowe's company: there is nothing at all anomalous about it, and for Henslowe's troupe, it signifies most immediately not any ambivalence on Jonson's part, but that female roles could thenceforth be played by an apprentice bricklayer.

Why did this clumsy use of the apprentice system constitute an advantageous arrangement for the acting companies? Why was it better than simply hiring a group of boys? One answer might be that the statutes governing apprenticeship were designed precisely to limit and control child labor, and though the professional theatres were not in fact covered by these regulations, the companies nevertheless found apprenticeship as defined by statute a system that worked for them. Whatever its specific practical merits, moreover, it worked more subtly by relating the work of acting to the crafts and professions, and thereby implicitly laying claim to their rights and privileges. But the derivation of this claim from the presence of boy apprentices in the company is worth pausing over: it is another instance of the patriarchal model at work in the culture, the assertion of position and authority through the deployment of legally obligated children. It also means that the companies were set up in such a way that the fact their plays could include female roles at all was dependent on a controlled social structure that had everything to do with mercantile and artisanal economics and nothing to do with theatre.

There is one exception to the generalization that boys could not be apprentice actors, and it is an instructive one. Under a royal patent, the children's companies were granted the right to impress boys into service – the logic of this was that the boys were to be trained as choristers, providing music for the royal chapel; they provided plays as well, but this was considered incidental. The boys legally served under an indenture of apprenticeship, and in a number of cases came to the company with their parents' authorization; this was an advantageous arrangement, a way of preparing a youth for a career as a professional musician. But the patent actually authorized the choirs to practice what amounted to legalized kidnapping, and in a remarkable suit in 1601, a gentleman named Henry Clifton brought an action in the Star Chamber against the director of the Blackfriars, Henry Evans, charging that Evans had removed his son and seven other boys from their grammar school to be forcibly apprenticed as actors. The Blackfriars at this period was really two companies, a chorus and a commercial theatrical enterprise; but the theatre operated under the same royal patent as the choir, or at least believed that it did. Clifton was able to enlist the Chancellor of the Exchequer on his side, and eventually his son was returned to him, though the rest of the boys seem to have remained with the troupe – to persuade the court to override the royal warrant in this particular instance, a great deal of influence was required. Evans was apparently felt to have overstepped his authority in this case, and was forbidden thenceforth to participate in the management of the company; this judgment, however, amounted to a slap on the wrist, since he returned to the Blackfriars shortly after – he was clearly being punished for tactlessness, rather than for a violation of the terms of the patent. The rules finally changed in 1606, when a new royal patent was issued specifically prohibiting the Blackfriars from using any impressed boys in plays.[21] What is notable here is both the class bias of the arrangement, and the dependence of the children's companies, at least in part, on enforced labor. The model for those troupes that operated under royal patents was as much the army as the guild.

If the adult companies were modeling themselves on the guilds, however, the relationship between the two was always an uneasy one. The persistent complaint of London commercial interests, that theatres are subversive, that the existence of theatres interferes with business, particularly that theatre seduces apprentices away from their craft, must have included a sense that the theatrical companies were in effect operating as unlicensed guilds, and even as antiguilds. There is also, surely, a doubly competitive edge to the complaint: theatre had been, for centuries in England, one of the most visible perquisites of the craftsmen's companies through the performance of mystery plays.

For the Elizabethan theatre to model itself on the guild has large ideological implications, which the mercantile world of Elizabethan London registers in its continual discomfort with and distrust of the new institution in its midst. For the acting companies, guild membership, in the context of Elizabethan London, was clearly more than an enabling mechanism for the hiring of boys. What other reasons might Jonson's theatrical colleagues have had for encouraging him to reaffirm his unpoetic status as a bricklayer? Belonging to a London guild conferred both privilege and protection. It meant that one had the freedom of the city – that one was a citizen with full rights to engage in business, trade or craft (in London, it conferred the right to engage in any trade, not simply the one in which one had been apprenticed). Since theatres were businesses, the freedom of the city was essential, though of course only the owners of the company had to possess it, and there were other ways of getting it than by membership in a guild – it could be bought, or inherited. But for a theatrical company to include a large number of free citizens also conferred on it a degree of respectability that must have seemed finally to put to rest the traditional actors' taint of vagrancy and marginality. I think it is most likely that the initial impulse of acting troupes toward the guild system came from this, its promise of respectability within the city structure, rather than from its utility as an enabling mechanism for theatrical apprentices.

Why then were the boys apprentices? Apprenticeship was certainly a convenient, if not essential, way of providing for the minors of the company. It benefited both the boys and their masters. The apprentice lived in his master's household, and was fed and clothed by him; in return, all wages due for the boy's services, with the exception of a small stipulated percentage, belonged to the master. For the actors, therefore, apprentices were good investments. This is not to say that the boys were simply being exploited: G. E. Bentley cites a number of cases in which the relationship was an explicitly familial one, with the boy being treated as an adoptive son, and being provided for as such in the master's will, even after the indenture period was over.

But here, too, practical considerations cannot have been the only ones. To problematize the question of why the boy actors were apprentices, we might rephrase it to ask what apprentices have to do with the representation of women. Sue-Ellen Case, in a brief and very provocative survey, notes that there are significant ways in which the relation of master and apprentice parallels that of husband and wife in a patriarchal society: the analogy between boys and women so prevalent in the disguise plots of Renaissance comedy is through the apprentice system asserted on an economic level as well.[22] The difference, of course, is that the boys complete their apprenticeships and end as members of the guild, men in a society of other men. It is always assumed that this was the model for the theatre as well, that the boys got their training playing women, but graduated to adult male roles. This sounds logical and may well be correct, but it is worth remarking how few documented instances there are of adult actors in the period who began by playing women: a search of Chambers and Bentley produces only two; T. J. King adds five more – this is for all the acting companies during the reigns of Elizabeth, James and Charles.[23] Are these seven normative? Evidence, of course, is hard to come by in such matters, and the meagerness may certainly be only of documentation, rather than of boy actresses-turned-actors; but we should at least consider the possibility that what we are dealing with is not simply a company organized according to categories of age, adults and adolescents, but two different classes of actors as well. *Did* boys who played women go on to play men? Some did, certainly, but what about the rest? As the system was structured, their apprenticeships legally entitled them to practice not as actors but as grocers, goldsmiths, bricklayers, etc., and in London to practice in any trade or craft they chose. Whether they decided to leave the company or not, this was what their expertise in the role of women legally prepared the boys to do.

Viewed in this light, it is less significant that the acting companies were all male than that they consisted of men and boys, masters and indentured servants, two asymmetrical classes of performers. So let us now rephrase our initial question once again: the question is not simply why boys played women; it is, more significantly, why *only* boys played women.[24] Verisimilitude is not the issue here, though it is almost invariably assumed to be: boys do not look any more like women than men do. It is important to bear in mind how time-bound the notion of what "women" look like is: boys have no facial hair, like women, but they also are slim-hipped and without breasts. There are also, needless to say, women with facial hair, or small breasts or slim hips, or with all of these (just as there are buxom men with large hips); but to judge from the evidence of portraits, the Elizabethan ideal, at least of aristocratic womanhood, was what we would call boyish and they called womanly: slim-hipped and flat-chested. Whether boys are thought to look like women or not depends on how society constructs the norm of womanliness; clearly it is in our interests to view boys as versions of men, but the Renaissance equally clearly sought the similitude in boys and women. What constitutes an acceptable representation of female behavior on the stage, moreover, is determined entirely by the conventions of that stage. Thomas Coryat was surprised to find that Italian actresses were quite as good at playing women as English boys were, and after the Restoration, when Edward Kynaston was playing female roles, he was declared by John Downes to be more convincingly female than any of his female colleagues.[25] For both these observers, realism was clearly not the major factor; the assumption is that the best actor makes the best woman. Spanish companies at various times used *both* boys and women in female roles, and in other all-male theatrical traditions, such as Kabuki and Noh, the age of the actor is as irrelevant as the gender: womanliness is simply a matter of acting.[26]

Why then did only boys play women? For Renaissance society the economic analogy between boys and women overlaid a more essential one: boys were, like women – but unlike men – acknowledged objects of sexual attraction for men. This is an element of the tradition that we prefer to elide or suppress, but, as I have observed, the homosexual, and particularly the pederastic, component of the Elizabethan erotic imagination is both explicit and for the most part surprisingly unproblematic. We might set beside Orlando's wooing of a youth he knows as Ganymede, the moment near the end of Middleton and Dekker's *The Roaring Girl* when Sebastian embraces his fiancée Mary, who is disguised as a boy, and remarks that he much prefers kissing her as a boy to kissing her as a girl:

MOLL. How strange this shows, one man to kiss another.
SEBASTIAN. I'd kiss such men to choose [i.e., by choice], Moll;
    Methinks a woman's lip tastes well in a doublet. (4.1.45–7)

The assumptions behind this preference are also clearly present in *As You Like It* and *Twelfth Night*, though they are never made explicit. The love of men for boys is all but axiomatic in the period; and despite fulminations in theological and legal contexts against the abominable crime of sodomy, most of what men and boys could do with each other did not constitute sodomy, and it was, as we have seen, a crime that was hardly ever prosecuted.

This is not to say that sex in itself is unproblematic in the period; but it is a problem with women as well as with men, and if we can judge from the evidence of Shakespeare's sonnets, despite all the age's heavy rhetoric about the monstrous unnameable crime against nature, the problem of sex between men involves a good deal less anxiety. The difficulties of homosexual intercourse, as the sonnets present them, are technical, not moral: "But since she pricked thee out for women's pleasure, / Mine be thy love, and thy love's use their treasure." Whatever the sexual dynamics implied here – they are, at best, terminally ambiguous – the poem, as Eve Sedgwick shrewdly remarks, assures the lover that it is perfectly all right to go on being passionately in love with the young man.[27] "Paederastice," E. K. similarly assures the reader of the January eclogue of Spenser's *Shepherd's Calendar*, "is much to be preferred before gynerastice, that is, the love which enflameth men with lust toward womankind."[28]

But what has all this to do with women – not with the representation of women, but with women themselves? The boy player was apparently as much an object of erotic attraction for women as for men: Pandarus and Cressida agree that Troilus has "not past three or four hairs on his chin" (1.2.105); Rosalind and Celia comment on Orlando's extreme youth (1.2.139ff.); Venus calls

Adonis "more lovely than a man, / More white and red than doves or roses are" (9–10). I have observed that to call the Elizabethan stage a male preserve is only narrowly correct – London theatre, like London itself, was a place of unusual freedom for women. Foreign visitors remark on the fact that women attend plays unescorted and unmasked, and all the sources agree that a large part of the audience were women. What *was* the place of women in the English Renaissance theatre? Standard history implies that until the Restoration women were banned from the stage, but in fact this is not the case; there were no statutes whatever relating to the matter. Hence, as we have seen, the occasional presence of French, Italian and even English actresses in Tudor, Jacobean and Caroline England; performers whose existence is elided from our construction of the English Renaissance theatre because it is inconvenient. And here once again the apprentice system provides a striking and unexpected analogy.

Standard history holds that the guilds were an all-male preserve, and that women could not be apprentices or guild members. This would be an especially useful fact if it were true, because the theatre then could be seen as a true mirror of the guild system. But standard history is wrong. The economic historian K. D. M. Snell, in a chapter of his book *Annals of the Labouring Poor* entitled "The Apprenticeship of Women," observes that although female apprenticeship is documented from the fifteenth century onward, and was relatively commonplace in the early seventeenth century, most historians absolutely deny its existence – "seemingly," he tactfully remarks, "through its incompatibility with prevailing judgements on the domestic roles of women."[29] The group of erring historians he cites includes a couple whom literary scholars regularly cite as oracles of historical truth: Lawrence Stone and E. P. Thompson.

Snell reports statistics that are absolutely astonishing: records survive of women in fifteenth-century London as full apprentices and guild members in the silk trade; in the fifteenth and sixteenth centuries the statutes of the masons' and carpenters' guilds are addressed to "systeren and bretheren"; until late in the seventeenth century women, in one place or another, were admitted into practically every English trade or guild. Women did not, moreover, limit their efforts to ladylike pursuits: in Chester, in 1575, there were five women blacksmiths. Elsewhere, women were armourers, bootmakers, printers, pewterers, goldsmiths, farriers, and so forth (Snell's list is a great deal longer), and they pursued these trades not as wives, widows, or surrogates, but as fully independent, legally responsible craftspersons. This point needs especially to be stressed, since a common modern way of ignoring the presence of women in the Renaissance workforce is to claim that they were there only as emanations of absent or dead husbands: this is not the case. The *percentage* of female apprentices is especially notable, for a practice that Lawrence Stone and E. P. Thompson believe did not exist. In Southampton, for example, at the beginning of the seventeenth century, 48 percent – almost half – the apprentices were women.[30]

There is, in short, nothing in the statutes relating to the guilds excluding women from apprenticeship, or limiting guild membership to men; nor were guilds, in the period we are concerned with, and indeed long after, ever so limited. The fact that the presence of women in the guild system declined markedly (it dropped, in Southampton, during the course of the seventeenth century to 9 percent) was, like the fact that there were no English actresses on the Elizabethan and early Stuart stage, a matter of social convention, not statute.[31] Presumably, as long as the labor force was small enough for women to be needed in it, the guild system accommodated them. When they started to represent competition to men (when, for example, in the seventeenth century the crafts guilds became a viable professional option for the younger sons of gentry) women were gradually either eased out, or eased into such clearly gender-linked crafts as the needle trades. To know whether this might constitute a model for the development of the all-male stage we would have to be able to compare the structure of early sixteenth-century theatrical companies with those from the middle of the century, something that the surviving evidence does not permit us to do. But the situation in both the guilds and the theatre confirms Joan Kelly's thesis that medieval women enjoyed more rights and had considerably more mobility than their Renaissance descendants – rights that, in the guilds, persisted much longer than they did in other areas of English society.

Though once again, not in as many other areas as modern historians have claimed: Patricia Crawford stunned the members of a recent conference of Early Modern historians by pointing out that a study of the voting registers shows that in certain parts of the country, women had been regularly voting in parliamentary elections during the seventeenth century into the 1650s at least, despite the fact that, according to Lord Chief Justice Coke, women were not legally entitled to vote.[32] This being the case, it becomes especially important not simply to assume that women were excluded from all areas of public life, and to look closely at those endeavors in which they did in fact participate, whether we believe they were legally empowered to do so or not. For the world of London, the public theatre should be considered a prime example. As Jean Howard observes,

To go to the theatre was, in short, to be positioned at the crossroads of cultural change and contradiction – and this seems to me particularly true for the middle-class female playgoer, who by her practices was calling into question the "place" of woman, perhaps more radically than did Shakespeare's fictions of cross-dressing.[33]

What did women enjoy about a theatre we find misogynistic? I have already suggested certain kinds of answers: plays about love matches are especially powerful fantasies of freedom in a patriarchal society, for women even more than for men; and the positive side of cuckoldry plots from the woman's perspective is the conviction that her sexuality is powerful and attractive, threatening to husbands, and under her own control: the point is made explicitly in Portia and Nerissa's ring trick at the end of *The Merchant of Venice*. This moment was largely ignored in critical treatments of the play until quite recently; but in 1980 Leonard Tennenhouse and in 1987 Lisa Jardine and Karen Newman built around the episode readings of the play that may be taken as manifestos for this generation's *Merchant of Venice*, challenging a critical history in which the play concludes with divine harmony and the joys of marriage.[34] The episode is, once one notices it, genuinely disruptive, pitting friendship against love, and leaving the conflict significantly unresolved. Its consistent elision from the history of criticism is not a matter of simple de-emphasis or dismissal. It has been, like Viola the eunuch and Rosalind the catamite, all but invisible.

Here, briefly, is the plot: at the conclusion of the trial scene, Portia and Nerissa, disguised as young men, demand as their recompense for saving Antonio's life the rings they have given Bassanio and Gratiano as love tokens and promises of marriage. Their fiancés object: they have sworn to wear the rings. The youths produce some heavy rhetoric about the monstrousness of ingratitude, Antonio lends his support, and the men unhappily give up the rings. When they return to Portia and Nerissa, now in their own persons, and reveal that the rings have been given to two youths as the price of an overwhelming debt of gratitude, the women feign outrage, accuse the men of faithlessness, and declare that they will consider themselves thenceforth relieved of the burden of fidelity to their husbands.

What is the point of this strange and discordant conclusion to a play that seemed to have resolved its problems in the containment of Shylock and the marriages of Portia and Bassanio, Lorenzo and Jessica? It could be a salutary point, reminding us that in this world there are no absolutes, that however steadfast we believe we will be to our vows, there are situations in which we will inevitably break them. In the circumstances of Antonio's trial, Bassanio was not wrong to give up the ring; Portia set up a test for him that she knew he was bound to fail. But the failure could lead the play to a great humane moral, that there are always extenuating circumstances, that the good isn't single, or isn't always clearly visible, urging us to be patient of our own and others' failings – demonstrating to us at last, as nothing else in the play does, that the quality of mercy is not strained. But the final revelation of Portia's and Nerissa's disguising evokes no such reassurance. The play ends not with the heavenly harmony that opens the final act, but, in its last moments, with threats and fears of a justified cuckoldry, combined, moreover, with a startling pederastic fantasy. In another one of those invisible moments, Gratiano conceives of his wedding night in terms of being in bed with the young man to whom he gave Nerissa's ring:

> were the day come, I should wish it dark
> Till I were couching with the doctor's clerk.
> Well, while I live I'll fear no other thing
> So sore as keeping safe Nerissa's ring –

"ring" being not simply the love token, but a word for both the vagina and the anus (of which "ring" is a literal translation): even sexually, Nerissa and the doctor's clerk are equivalents and alternatives. These are the last lines of the play: the women's charade has given Portia and Nerissa something to hold over their husbands forever, something to ensure that in marriage the men can never be certain of their wives' chastity and the women always have the upper hand. The patriarchal structure is always in place, always threatened.

If we resist the impulse simply to dismiss this as a pointless joke the women play on the men, with no larger implications, but focus instead on the anxieties it expresses, as criticism has begun to do, it is part of a fantasy of female sexual power that is difficult to read as humane or benevolent. It sets the demands of marriage not only against those of friendship, but, more dangerously, against those of gratitude, and in a culture of clientage, as this is, ingratitude is the primal sin – as it still is in Milton's version of the Fall, that exemplary case of a man required to choose between loyalty to his wife or to his patron, and making the wrong choice. Portia is, after all, in the most literal sense Antonio's gift to Bassanio: as Edward II finding a wife for his beloved Gaveston, and James I arranging marriages for his favorites Carr and Villiers make clear, a wife is the supreme gift of male friendship, not at all a repudiation of it. Portia, however, engineers a marriage that does constitute a repudiation of male friendship; and it is to the point that she has to pose as a man in order to do so. People who are disturbed by the depiction of Portia in this episode – if we take both it and the Renaissance patronage system seriously, the play's conclusion can be seen as powerfully misogynistic – are being offended by the extent to which the women in this play are represented precisely as acting like men; and the domineering – or, as the age significantly put it, *masculine* – woman was in this culture both a figure of fun and deeply destabilizing. Indeed, Tennenhouse maintains that in *The Merchant of Venice*, "Shakespeare has created a problem which can only be resolved by a transvestite."[35]

But we need to look further than interpretation, beyond the plots: asking what Renaissance women would have liked about such a play is certainly to ask the wrong question. There are many reasons for going to theatre, and very few of them have anything to do with the texts of plays. We need to ask structural questions – not only why women were excluded from a stage that two generations earlier had apparently employed them unproblematically, but what kind of freedom the social dimension of theatre represented for Renaissance women; and more speculatively, whether there was anything in the transvestite theatre itself that might have been positively appealing to a Renaissance female audience. This is a matter in which our own responses to what have become our classic texts will be very

77

uncertain guides; we naturally concentrate our attention on Shakespeare, but most of what the Renaissance stage presented was not Shakespeare. And recent attempts to read back from how we feel about boys dressed as women to what Renaissance women "must" have felt strike me as utterly unpersuasive, not only method-ologically.

A better starting point seems to me Lisa Jardine's contention that "playing the woman's part – male effeminacy – is an act for a male audience's appreciation."[36] There is ample evidence, from the Jonson of *Epicoene* to Dame Edna Everedge that this is true; but is there anything in the act for a female audience as well? Renaissance literature is in fact rich in plots involving male transvestism in which women are deeply implicated, not only as the cause, but sometimes directly as the instigators. Cleopatra, for example, amuses herself by dressing the drunken Antony in her garments:

> the next morn
> Ere the ninth hour I drunk him to his bed;
> Then put my tires and mantles on him, whilst
> I bore his sword Philippan. (2.5.20ff.)

In doing so, she replicates the behavior of Queen Omphale with Antony's ancestor Hercules, commanded by the gods to serve her as her slave in whatever capacity she wished. Omphale set him to doing women's household work; in some versions of the story this was intended simply as a humiliation, but in others it was a device to keep him by her side, and Hercules fell deeply in love with her. Ancient representations of the couple show Hercules in Omphale's garments and holding her distaff, while she wears his lion skin and bears his club.

Sidney's *Arcadia* includes a transvestite episode that also alludes to the classic Herculean model, and moralizes it in a way that emphasizes both the arbitrary element in gender construction and the deep ambiguities implicit in cross-dressing.[37] The heroes of this epic romance, the warrior friends Pyrocles and Musidorus, have fallen in love with two sisters, the princesses Pamela and Philocleia. Pyrocles, in order to gain access to Philocleia, disguises himself as an Amazon warrior. Musidorus comes upon him in the forest, and is appalled at the transformation he sees. He urges Pyrocles to give up the disguise, effeminate and unworthy of a soldier. But Pyrocles defends himself with some surprisingly forceful Platonic logic. He says that it is in the nature of love to imitate the beloved; that since women are virtuous, imitating them cannot be vicious; and that no human being's virtue is complete unless it encompasses the virtue of women as well as men. Pyrocles is, in short, realizing Aristophanes' fable in Plato's *Symposium* in which humankind as originally created was a double creature, subsequently separated by the gods in envy of its perfect happiness. This explains our deep desire for coupling, and Pyrocles is undertaking to reunite in himself the severed halves of the original humanity, to make his beloved literally a part of himself.

This argument baffles Musidorus, but it half persuades him, and he himself adopts the disguise of a menial shepherd in order to woo Philocleia's sister Pamela – transformations of gender and those of social class are here identified, prompted by the same impulse, as means to the same end. For a reader the incident is more baffling still. Are we intended to endorse Pyrocles' reasoning, and see in it the acting out of a Platonic allegory? Or is it merely an instance of the irrationality characteristically induced by love? The ambiguities of the scene are summed up in a visual emblem: Pyrocles wears a brooch engraved with the figure of Hercules bearing the distaff of Omphale; its motto is "Never more valiant." What does it mean? That Hercules is never more valiant than when he performs the tasks of Omphale? This labor, after all, was imposed on him by the gods, and his willingness to undertake it is an instance of his extraordinary piety. Or does it mean that having taken on the character of Omphale, having abandoned his manhood to the effeminating passion of love, Hercules will never more be valiant? The emblem embodies the traditional moral ambivalence of the Herculean hero, an ambivalence expressed here specifically through the double image of the dominating woman and the transvestite man.

For all its moral ambiguities, however, Pyrocles' ruse is an unqualified success. He takes the name Zelmane, his Amazonian disguise admits him to Philocleia's presence, and in due time he is lodged as fully in her affections as the most passionate lover could wish. Sidney's account of the growth of Philocleia's love confirms the claims made by Pyrocles in his Platonic justification of his cross-dressing:

> Then followed that most natural effect of conforming ones self to that, which she did like . . . so that as Zelmane did often eye her, she would often eye Zelmane; and as Zelmane's eyes would deliver a submissive, but vehement desire in their looke, she, though as yet she had not the desire in her, yet should her eyes answere in like pearcing kindnesse of a looke . . . till at the last (poore soule, ere she were aware) she accepted not onely the band, but the service; not only the signe, but the passion signified.[38]

The nature of love is to strive to be like the beloved; women are therefore best wooed by imitation. It is, indeed, precisely Pyrocles' ability to perform as a woman that persuades Philocleia to love him.

Is this tale of the extraordinary effectiveness of cross-dressing in love affairs really designed for the appreciation of male readers? Since the readership of romances was overwhelmingly female – Sidney's title, after all, is *The Countess of Pembroke's Arcadia* – this would, at the very least, constitute a large miscalculation. Indeed, almost a century later, at a time when women were regularly appearing on the English stage and constituted fair game for the attentions of male spectators, Nathaniel Lee warned the men in the audience of the consequence of luring female actors away from the stage and into domesticity. The theatre will return to using boys, and this will deprive men not only of the women on the stage, but more particularly of the women in the audience:

For we have vow'd to find a sort of Toys
Known to black Fryars, a Tribe of chopping*a* Boys.
If once they come, they'l quickly spoil your sport;
There's not one Lady will receive your Court:
But for the Youth in Petticoats run wild,
With oh the archest Wagg, the sweetest Child.
The panting Breasts, white Hands and little Feet
No more shall your pall'd thoughts with pleasure meet.[39]

Peter Stallybrass remarks that here "the threat to replace women with
boy actors is not imagined as a *general* loss but as a loss to the male
spectator alone. The female spectator, on the contrary, is imagined as
running wild after the 'Youth in Petticoats.' The boy actor is thus
depicted as particularly alluring to women."[40]

This is, no doubt, not at all what we believe women want, or
ought to want; and doubtless too there is a large element of fantasy
in Lee's warning, as there is in Sidney's and Shakespeare's transvestite
plots – there is no evidence that Sidney wore drag when he
undertook to woo Penelope Rich and Frances Walsingham. But the
fantasies extend well beyond Sidney, Shakespeare and Lee; they are
cultural ones, and have to do with the way the age constructs
femininity. To deny women a place in these fantasies is to deny them
their place in the culture. For a female audience, in a culture as
patriarchally stratified as that of Renaissance England, to see the
youth in skirts might be to disarm and socialize him in ways that
were specifically female, to see him not as a possessor or master, but
as companionable and pliable and one of them – as everything, in
fact, that the socialized Renaissance woman herself is supposed to be.
It strikes me that *Twelfth Night* provides just such a model in Olivia,
in love with the boy/girl/eunuch Cesario/Sebastian, "maid and
man" – she might, after all, have been paired off instead with the one
"real" man in the play, the fighter–pirate – and lover of boys –

a strapping

81

Antonio, who ends, like his namesake in *The Merchant of Venice*, coupled with no one. Falling in love with "real" men in Shakespeare is a dangerous matter: the model for it is provided in *Othello*.

One thing such moments certainly suggest, even for us, is the degree to which both gender and sexual desire, in any era, are socially and culturally constructed. This is true for both sexes; and women profit from these representations and are empowered by them precisely through that recognition. It is, after all, Omphale who dresses Hercules in her garments, Cleopatra who puts Antony into her tires and mantles. These are represented not as male stratagems, but as transformations that give women power and pleasure.

5

Masculine apparel

The emblem of Hercules and Omphale, however, has more prejudicial cultural implications than those elicited by Sidney from
Pyrocles' mythological cameo. The mythographer Alexander Ross
observes that "*Hercules* dishonoured all his former actions by doting
upon *Omphale*," and that therefore

it was not lawful for women to swear by *Hercules*, nor to enter into his temple:
this was a punishment laid upon that sex, for the insolency of Queen *Omphale*
over *Hercules*, in causing him so effeminately to serve her.[1]

The other side of male effeminacy was female masculinity, and the
identification of socially offensive behavior in women as
"masculine" constitutes one of the most commonplace of
Renaissance slippages – what Leontes in *The Winter's Tale* implies by
calling the argumentative Paulina "a mankind witch," not merely a
witch, the essence of feminine wickedness, but something even
worse, one who behaves like a man. In social contexts, the
complaint focused particularly on fashions in clothing, which were
construed as instances of cross-dressing. The *locus classicus* here is
King James's well-known admonition to the London clergy,
requiring them "to inveigh vehemently and bitterly in their sermons
against the insolency of our women, and their wearing of broad-
brimmed hats, pointed doublets, their hair cut short or shorn, and
some of them stillettos or poniards . . . adding withall that if pulpit
admonitions will not reform them he would proceed by another
course."[2] This admonition was directed against what was seen as a

masculine style of dress; but the ministers did not invariably understand the point of the royal injunction. "The Dean of Westminster [John Chamberlain reported] hath been very strict in his church against Ladies and gentlewomen about yellow ruffs, and would not suffer them to be admitted into any pew." Yellow ruffs being particularly stylish at that moment, the fashionable parishioners appealed at once to the king, who was obliged to explain that "his meaning was not for yellow ruffs, but for other man-like and unseemly apparel."[3]

What constitutes masculinity, however, in apparel as in everything else, is a matter of opinion. Plate 1 shows Paul van Somer's 1617 portrait of the queen in hunting costume, with broad-brimmed hat, short hair, pointed doublet – and yellow ruffs.[4] The picture, roughly contemporary with the king's expostulation, was painted for her, and shows her own palace of Oatlands in the background; it presents her as she wanted to see herself, as queen and huntress. The implications of the costume are revealed in the contemporaneous French term for a riding habit, *amazone*. Is the real object of King James's outburst, then, his wife's taste in fashion? The possibility is not inconceivable; husband and wife had few tastes in common, and by 1617 were maintaining both different households and different religions – indeed, Queen Anne's conversion to Roman Catholicism had been a problem for the king for two decades, even threatening to compromise his accession to the English throne. Man-like and unseemly clothes in this case would be an index to a much more dangerous kind of independence. And if every Englishman was a king in his own household, was every Englishwoman by the same token a version of the unmanageable queen?

Here is the same issue in reverse. Barnabe Riche, in his *Farewell to the Military Profession*, indicates as one of the major changes driving him from his calling the effeminization of the military:

Plate 1 Paul van Somer, *Anne of Denmark*, 1617.

It was my fortune to walk through the Strand towards Westminster, where I met one who came riding towards me . . . apparelled in a French ruff, a French cloak, French hose, and in his hand a great fan of feathers, bearing them up very womanly against the side of his face. And for that I had never seen any man wear them before that day, I began to think it impossible that there might be found a man so foolish as to make himself a scorn to the world, to wear so

Plate 2 Nicholas Hilliard, *Charles Blount, Lord Mountjoy, later Earl of Devonshire, c.* 1600.

womanish a toy, but rather thought it had been some shameless woman that had disguised herself like a man in our hose and our cloaks; for our doublets, gowns, caps, and hats they had got long ago.[5]

For comparison with Riche's description of unsuitable masculine fashion, plate 2 is a miniature of Lord Mountjoy, elaborately curled and earringed – this is the military hero who succeeded in the pacification of Ireland after Essex failed. Riche focuses his disapproval on the fan; to the best of my knowledge, no gentleman in the period had himself depicted with such an accessory, but the association of military and aristocratic masculinity with feathers is easy enough to document. Plate 3 shows a Polish horseman liberally furnished, and in plate 4 the feathered hat is an important element in the lavish costume of George Villiers, on his creation as Marquis of Buckingham (it is even more important in the portrait of the Prince of Wales in plate 8, below). Riche's greater point, about what he sees as the feminization of the military, is amply attested by any number of other portraits, ranging from George Clifford, Earl of Cumberland, the Queen's champion, shown in plate 5 in jousting costume, to Essex himself, in plate 6, as he was portrayed after his victory at Cadiz. Any of these images might do for the "certain lord" who so outrages Hotspur on the battlefield, "neat and trimly dressed, / Fresh as a bridegroom . . . / perfumèd like a milliner."[6] Riche's diagnosis of the new social disease places its etiology securely in heterosexuality, observing that the fashion is adopted "to please gentlewomen." The assumption here is the same as that of Pyrocles disguising himself as an Amazon to woo Philocleia: women are won by imitation; what they want are versions of themselves. Riche's version of heterosexuality is literally homoerotic.

But of course Clifford, Essex and Mountjoy are not simply gentleman soldiers; they are the equivalent of four-star generals, and all these portraits are documents in the creation of a set of idealized public selves. The essential question here is not so much what constitutes masculinity or femininity, but what constitutes glamor in the representation of the stars of the 1590s. Plate 7 shows the most widely circulated portrait of King James's elder son Prince Henry, who saw himself as a military hero. He is presented as manly and athletic, practicing at the lance. Plate 8, on the other hand, is his investiture portrait as Prince of Wales, painted only a year earlier – the lace collar, the luxuriantly feathered hat (three

Ein Polonischer Hofiuncker . Nobilis Polonus. 27. S

Plate 3 Abraham de Bruyn, Polish rider, 1600.

Plate 4 William Larkin, (attrib.) *George Villiers,*
1st Duke of Buckingham, c. 1616.

Plate 5 Nicholas Hilliard, *George Clifford, 3rd Earl of Cumberland*, c. 1590.

Plate 6 Marcus Gheeraerts the Younger, *Robert Devereux,*
2nd Earl of Essex, c. 1596.

HENRICVS PRINCEPS

Plate 7 William Hole, *Henry Frederick, Prince of Wales*, from Michael
Drayton, *Poly-Olbion* (London, 1613).

Plate 8 Robert Peake, *Henry Frederick, Prince of Wales.*

ostrich feathers were an attribute of the royal office), the pompoms on the shoes, the richly embroidered doublet and breeches, the dainty gloves, the accentuation of the hips with even a suggestion of a farthingale, all indicate how undifferentiated with regard to gender the idealizations of fashion were in the period. It is clear that these two representations of the heir to the throne do not contradict each other. Just to make it even clearer, here is some mythographic evidence: two plates from the popular mid-sixteenth-century iconology of Georg Pictor. Plate 9 is Pallas Athena, the martial goddess – the owl at her feet indicates that the woodcut was originally intended to depict her. But Pictor used the same image for Hercules, merely changing the heading (plate 10). Doubtless this conjunction has as much to do with the exigencies of early printing as with the interchangeability of genders in the Renaissance; but it is also clear that in the representation of heroism and divinity, as of royalty, gender was not an exclusive category.

A case in point, and in many ways a defining *locus classicus* for the Renaissance representation of the hero, is found in portraits of Alexander the Great. As Julius Held observes, "A very common ancient Alexander-coin showed on one side the helmeted head of Pallas Athena. Since no inscription is found on this side of the coin, while Alexander's name appears on the reverse, the youthful if martial head of Athena, its long curls included, was accepted as a portrait of Alexander himself."[7] Both François I and his son Henri II made exemplary use of the virtues of double gender by having themselves depicted in dresses (plates 11 and 12).[8] François' image is accompanied by an explanatory motto: the king is a Mars in war, a Minerva or Diana in peace. By his son's time, the explanation was apparently unnecessary. Plate 13 indicates the degree to which such images could be seen as directly erotic, Cornelis van Haarlem's sumptuous *Venus and Adonis* (1619): save for the slight accentuation of Venus's breasts, the two figures are mirror images of each other,

Plate 9 Georg Pictor, Minerva, from *Apotheoseos* (Basel, 1558).

down even to the pearl earring, and it appears that the same model
was used for both hero and heroine.

Gender, moreover, is not the only relevant issue here. Barnabe
Riche's scorn is directed at the sartorial pretensions of an ordinary
gentleman. Would he take the same line about Essex, or Mountjoy,

HERCVLIS IMAGO.

Plate 10   Georg Pictor, Hercules, from *Apotheoseos* (Basel, 1558).

or the Prince of Wales? Let us return to Queen Anne in her hunting
dress: is the king's indictment of "man-like and unseemly apparel"
really directed at her? Perhaps; but perhaps too the politics of gender
is more complex than this. For all the pulpit rhetoric about the evils
of cross-dressing, sumptuary legislation said nothing about the

Plate 11 Niccolo Bellin da Modena, *Transvestite Portrait of François I*, 1545.

Plate 12 Medal of Henri II as transvestite, 1552.

wearing of sexually inappropriate garments. It was concerned with violations of the sartorial badges of class, not those of gender. Tradesmen and their wives were enjoined from wearing the satins and velvets of aristocrats, people below the rank of gentry were limited to clothing made of certain kinds of wool and other plain cloth (the legislation, not surprisingly, works only in one direction; it does not prohibit the gentry from wearing frieze jerkins). The statutes were finally acknowledged to be unenforceable in the civil law, and were repealed in 1604, but this only complicated matters further: it did not mean that there were no longer any sumptuary regulations, it only transferred the jurisdiction over questions of appropriate dress, as an issue of public morality, from the criminal courts to the ecclesiastical ones, where the guidelines were much less clear.

Insofar as sumptuary legislation in the period generalizes about

Plate 13 Cornelis van Haarlem, *Venus and Adonis*, 1619.

women, it insists on just the distinctions the king refuses to make: it declares that all women are not the same; what is proper dress for ladies is not proper for women of the middle class – indeed, it says the same of men, and thereby declines to distinguish the sexes. King James did not have much use for women, but perhaps the point of his reproach is really the same as the point of van Somer's painting: that the queen sets her own style; and that what is appropriate for the queen is not appropriate for other women. The royal outrage would be, in this reading, against presuming to imitate the style of royalty, and thereby encroaching on the prerogatives of the crown – a danger the king throughout his reign saw as ubiquitous.

This may well be giving the king too much credit. But the idea that masculine dress could serve as a potent mode of female idealization is clear from plate 14, showing Elizabeth rallying her troops before the anticipated invasion of the Armada in 1588. The engraving was done in the 1630s, and as Susan Frye has shown, it is pure fantasy: there is no evidence that Elizabeth wore armor on this or any other occasion; but the image of the late queen as an Amazon – or, depending on your point of view, a virago – served as an effective rebuke to the effeminate Charles I, who was felt by his critics to be controlled by his French Catholic wife.[9]

What, then, are the limits of social imitation? It is in the nature of social hierarchies that the rules descend from above, and this is as true of the laws of fashion as of those of commerce and domestic arrangements. Theatre was under aristocratic and ultimately royal patronage, but it constituted both an obvious violation of the sumptuary laws – it presented middle-class actors and working-class apprentices dressed as aristocrats – and a powerful stimulus to society as a whole to violate them. Polemicists from Philip Stubbes to William Prynne record in compulsive and fascinated detail the ungodly finery characteristic of London theatre audiences, and Sir Henry Wotton's reaction to Shakespeare's *Henry VIII* at the Globe, that it was "sufficient in truth within a while to make greatness very familiar if not ridiculous,"[10] puts the case against the imitation of royalty, whether by players or audiences, succinctly. Marion Trousdale, in a brilliant discussion of the interrelations of sumptuary legislation, fashion and the stage, quotes the correspondence of Philip Gawdy, resident in London from the 1580s until his death in 1617, who moves in the world of the court and the City, frequents

Plate 14 Thomas Cecil, *Elizabeth I in Armor*, c. 1630.

the playhouses, observes the fashions of the great and sends stylish apparel home to his family in Norfolk. With a shipment of clothing he writes to his sister that "I can assure you that both the queen and all the gentlewomen at the court wear the very fashion of your tough [i.e. stiffened] taffeta gown with an open wired sleeve and such a cut, and it is now the newest fashion."[11] Fashion, even in Elizabethan Norfolk, descends directly from the queen.

To imitate the queen and the court aristocracy, however, was, as Trousdale shows, in the most literal way also to imitate the theatre. In 1572 Thomas Giles (or Gylles), a haberdasher,[12] lodged a complaint against the Office of the Queen's Revels. He charges that the Yeoman of the Revels leases out masquing costumes that are the property of the crown to "all sort of persons"; that these courtly clothes are then worn not only "in the court," but "into the city or country," where they are subjected to "the great press of people and foulness both of the way and weather and soil of the wearers, who for the most part be of the meanest sort of men, to the great discredit of the same apparel, which afterward is to be showed before her highness and to be worn by them of great calling." The point of this complaint is not a demand for enforcement of the sumptuary laws; Giles claims his concern is for the welfare of the costumes, not for the social hierarchy. But his real purpose, as he readily admits, is to protect his own business from royal competition – he too has fancy dress for hire, and he is, he says, "greatly hindered of his living hereby . . . having apparel to let and cannot so cheaply let the same as her highness's masques be let."[13] The fact that the Queen's Revels could do a thriving business in renting out aristocratic clothes at cut rates to "the meanest sort of men" indicates both what kind of investment the culture had in the semiotics of clothing and how little regulations about who could wear what represented social practice.

For us, the prime instance of the misrepresentations of costume in the period are the innumerable disguises that constitute so large an element in the plots of Elizabethan drama. If costume was essential to theatre, the wrong costume was quintessential. This is a case, moreover, where clothes really do make the man: as we have observed, there are scarcely a handful of instances in which anyone sees through a disguise in English Renaissance drama. In the England of Elizabeth, the most highly charged misrepresentations were those of class, hence the legislation against wearing clothes that admitted one to an undeserved place in the hierarchy, and hence also the endemic flouting of the legislation. On the stage, however, the egregious misrepresentations are those of gender, the playing of women by boys, and within the drama the playing of boys by women. But this practice too was, as we have seen, just as thoroughly naturalized in Renaissance England as the violation of the semiotics of class: the only people who found it reprehensible were those for whom theatre itself was reprehensible.

That the analogy between boys and women was naturalized does not imply that boys are substitutes for women; it implies just the opposite: both are treated as a medium of exchange within the patriarchal structure, and both are (perhaps in consequence) constructed as objects of erotic attraction for adult men. Boys and women are not in competition in this system; they are antithetical not to each other, but to men. This is clear, for example, in the passage from Lady Mary Wroth's *Urania* to which I have already alluded, describing a lover seeing his mistress in another man's arms, and observing that he was "unmoveable, no further wrought than if he had seen a delicate play-boy act a loving woman part, and knowing him a boy, liked only his action."[14] The accuracy of the generalization is not the issue here; there is ample evidence that homoerotic pederasty was a strong element in the erotic life of Renaissance England, and Mary Wroth to the contrary notwithstanding, it is demonstrable that many men in the period did find boys sexually exciting. But the point is that Wroth does not see the boy as threatening – and it should probably be added that the lover in *Urania* is being duped: he *ought* to be jealous; he is a fool not to be, the equivalent of a cuckold. (It is at least arguable that this reflects on Wroth's own sexual complacency.) When Lear issues his warning about the untrustworthiness of a boy's love, he is asserting a commonplace (that is, falling in love with boys is commonplace in this society); and like the proverbial wisdom declaring the unreliability of women, it is asserted in the ultimate interest of defining and stabilizing the nature not of boys and women, but of men.

What allows boys to be substituted for women in the theatre, however, is not anything about the genital nature of boys and women, but precisely the costume, and more particularly, cultural assumptions about costume. Orsino's love for the youth he knows as Cesario is paralleled by Antonio's love for Sebastian, the youth he knows as Roderigo, and despite the fact that there were no twins in Shakespeare's company, the two are represented on stage as being indistinguishable – an effect achieved, then as now, by simply dressing them in identical costumes. As Viola says, Sebastian "went / Still in this fashion, color, ornament, / For him I imitate" (3.4.361–3). Twins are people who *dress* alike. Jonson was, characteristically, more of a realist: he told Drummond that "he had an intention to have made a play like Plautus' *Amphitrio*, but left it off for that he could never find two so like others that he could persuade the spectators they were one."[15] (It is worth observing, in view of recent claims about the symbolic efficacy of doubling on the Renaissance stage, that neither Shakespeare nor Jonson considered it of any use whatever in the representation of twins.) The flummery at the conclusion of *Twelfth Night* about the impossibility of proceeding with the marriage of Orsino and Viola (and therefore the impossibility of concluding the plot) until Viola's clothes have been found declares in the clearest possible way that, whatever Viola says about the erotic realities of her inner life, she is not a woman unless she is dressed as one. Even here, it is a *particular* costume that matters, her *own* dress that was left with the sea captain: this is the dress that *is* Viola. The costume is the real thing; borrowing a dress from Olivia or buying a new one to get married in are not offered by the play as options. Clothes make the woman, clothes make the man: the costume is of the essence.

When Prospero tempts Stefano and Trinculo to their destruction with a closet full of "glistering apparel," he invokes a central cultural topos. Caliban declares the garments to be "trash"; but they are trash only because the conspirators are not yet entitled to wear them – robes of office, aristocratic finery, confirm and legitimate authority, they do not confer it. There is obviously, however, a widespread conviction in the culture that they do. Caliban may well be revealing here just how much of an outsider he is – the costumes, after all, are Prospero's. Prospero himself invests his cape with the enabling power of his magic: "Lie there, my art" (1.2.25). Analogously, the wardrobe of Henslowe's company included "a robe for to go invisible,"[16] asserting in a culturally specific manner how powerfully garments determined the way one was to be seen, and not seen. These fictions, moreover, reflect an economic reality: the theatre company has its largest investment, its major property, in its costumes; and the costumes are for the most part the real cast-off clothes of real aristocrats. As the legitimating emblems of authority, these garments possess a kind of social reality within the culture that the actors, and indeed much of their audience, can never hope to have.[17]

6

Mankind witches

We have seen that one way of viewing the transvestite actor of Shakespeare's stage is as a response to a large cultural anxiety, a manifestation of the audience's, and ultimately of the culture's, desire for a disarmed woman. Alternatively, we have seen it as just the opposite, a performative construction that both reveals the malleability of the masculine and empowers the feminine, enabling the potential masculinity of women to be realized and acknowledged, if safely contained within the theatre's walls. And insofar as actors perform roles that are provided for them, and depend for their livelihood on satisfying audiences, this account is probably satisfactory as far as it goes. Admittedly it does not go very far – it does not, for example, explain why English theatres differed from those on the Continent in this respect; but perhaps it does not need to: it might be sufficient to observe that different societies have different ways of responding to common cultural anxieties. Italy executed sodomites while England on the whole ignored them.

Such an account of the transvestite stage, however, elides the performer: in a larger context, it must be to the point that there are people in this culture who want, or are willing, to play such roles. Boy actors are, for us, the most noticeable instance, but for the culture itself, they were the smallest part of a large social phenomenon; and it was primarily women who were seen as exemplifying the dangers of cross-dressing. We might even say, paradoxically, that boys in drag are a special case of women in drag. The most famous instance in the period is Mary Frith (the model for

Middleton and Dekker's *Roaring Girl*), a woman who presented herself, defined her identity, as a transvestite, and was accepted as such – accepted, that is, as a transvestite, not as a man. The disguise here is no disguise, but at most an open secret; Mary Frith's self-presentation is on one level only an extreme instance of the masculine attire for women that so notoriously constituted high fashion in the period. No actual boundary is crossed in such performances – the women do not represent themselves as anything but women, even if they are attacked as being mannish. Moreover, although there is a good deal of violent rhetoric about the heinousness of such cross-dressing, no sumptuary laws were ever enacted relating to such cases: it was not illegal for women to dress in male attire. Sumptuary laws regulated violations of social class, workers dressing as gentry, tradespeople dressing as aristocrats, not violations of gender. Why then do women want to present themselves as mannish in a culture that seems to reprehend such behavior, and why, if the behavior is really seen as reprehensible, does it remain legal, and thereby, in some significant sense – the literal sense *must* be significant – legitimate?

The fears of a patriarchal society about the power of women, localized in sexual power, are often cited to account for a characteristically misogynistic tone to public discourse in the English Renaissance, and anxiety about women, summed up perhaps most memorably in the title of John Knox's collective libel *A First Blast of the Trumpet Against the Monstrous Regiment of Women* (1558), is unquestionably an important element in the culture. The gender categories as defined for Tudor readers by Sir Thomas Elyot in 1531 remained clear and firm throughout the age:

A man in his natural perfection is fierce, hardy, strong in opinion, covetous of glory, desirous of knowledge, appetiting by generation to bring forth his sem-blable [i.e. eager for offspring]. The good nature of a woman is to be mild, timorous, tractable, benign, of sure remembrance, and shamefast.[1]

What is monstrous to Knox is the confusion of the categories – the tirade is a warning of the evils sure to follow from the accession of women to the thrones of Scotland and England, queens occupying the proper place of kings. Even in less apocalyptic contexts, the charge that women have usurped the place of men, or the fear that they will do so, is so commonplace as to constitute a moral topos in the period. But the danger of treating Renaissance misogyny as a cultural constant is the tendency to naturalize it. Whose interests did misogynist discourse serve? In the largest sense, patriarchal societies are primarily concerned with the management of the class structure, and only by extension, or as an aspect of this, with the management of women – the analogy between servants and women extends well beyond the apprentice boys of the Elizabethan stage. Indeed, the oxymoron by which the most successful English acting company chose to identify itself after 1603, "Gentlemen the King's Servants," seems designed to insist precisely on the socially transgressive nature of theatre itself, the medium in which .class boundaries are systematically violated and sumptuary laws flouted, as lower-class actors wear aristocratic clothing and mime greatness. But as the long history of royal and noble patronage of the stage indicates, the transgressiveness is generally more serviceable than threatening to those in power, not least, paradoxically, in the theatre's ability to imagine and rewrite the nature of power, or masculinity, or the very notion of subjectivity itself. And despite the fact that the violation of gender boundaries in the course of this enterprise seemed a critical issue only to marginal elements in the culture, the issue is not marginal – in this context, it is of the essence. The transvestite actor was indispensable to Renaissance England; but (or, perhaps, therefore) the figure was never fully naturalized. He was essential precisely as a construct, always available to interrogate, unsettle, reinterpret the norms, which were always conceived to be unstable – the interrogation, indeed, was an essential part of the never-ending attempt at stabilization.

Beyond the theatre, transvestism was far more obviously a potent issue, highly charged but so hopelessly nonspecific that King James's attack on masculine attire for women could result in the banishment of yellow ruffs from the churches of Westminster. The slippage between sumptuary display and gender transgression was clearly not limited to the mind of the Dean of Westminster: modern critics regularly do the same conflation when they assume that Elizabethan sumptuary laws regulated cross-dressing. The statutes, as I have said, do not touch on the matter. It is to the point that in England, French and Italian fashionable male style was considered effeminate: transvestism is, to a large degree, in the eye of the beholder.

It is precisely that eye with which we are concerned. Why was the female boy unproblematic, while the image of the masculine woman was so highly charged? The answer cannot be found in gynecological tracts or sumptuary admonitions, which in effect merely restate the question. Why represent men as women and women as men? We have seen that the cross-dressing that does not represent but is represented in so much Renaissance drama, the transvestism of Viola, Rosalind, Portia and Nerissa, expresses a wide variety of patriarchal anxieties, and that these have more to do with the authority of the father within the family structure, with issues relating to inheritance, the transfer of property and the contracting of alliances, than with gender or sexuality. These anxieties are a function of the patriarchal structure itself, responding to those elements in society that are its essential currency. As Karen Newman aptly puts it, "Managing femininity so as to insure the reproduction of the commonwealth, great and small, was a significant ideological feature of early modern England."[2] Women and children (and the society has an investment in representing women as perpetual children) become the cultural metonyms for the working classes generally – all those elements that must be controlled if the patriarchy is to survive.

The masculine woman in such a context would be a singularly

threatening symbol, or at least she should be if patriarchy is to account for her. How threatening in fact was she? There is no single answer, and the multiple ones are remarkably inconsistent. Witches, though epitomizing what was conceived as a specifically female propensity to wickedness, were also regularly accused of being either unfeminine or androgynous, as Banquo observes at his first sight of them in *Macbeth*:

> You should be women,
> And yet your beards forbid me to interpret
> That you are so. (1.3.45–7)

The specifically and dangerously female here expresses itself through masculine attributes. Four years after *Macbeth*, however, Ben Jonson employed a coven of witches to provide the antimasque for *The Masque of Queens*, his celebration of female heroism and virtue. So conceived, witches and queens are two sides of a single coin; the fearsome and the admirable share the same attributes of masculine vigor, strength and independence – the witches are the queens in reverse, literally, etymologically "preposterous." Indeed, in the structure of the masque, the witches, defining themselves as "faithful opposites / To fame and glory," *produce* their heroic antitheses. And as with the image of Queen Elizabeth in armor, it is precisely the masculinity of the queens that constitutes their virtue: they are not Elyot's "mild, timorous, tractable" creatures, but armed and aggressive. Plate 15 is Inigo Jones's costume design for the Countess of Bedford, who danced the role of Penthesilea, Queen of the Amazons: what was anathema to John Knox served Jonson and Jones as a heroic trope.[3] The epic power of gender confusion is exemplified in Milton's vision of England purified and revitalized as "a noble and puissant nation rousing herself like a strong man after sleep, and shaking her invincible locks."[4] The tragedy of Samson betrayed by his exemplary effeminacy, with his invincible locks as the signifier of both his power and the power of women over him, is only a step beyond.

Plate 15 Inigo Jones, costume design for Penthesilea,
Masque of Queens, 1609.

Even as the age defined its gender boundaries, it also continually – one might almost say compulsively – produced figures who overstepped or violated them. In literature, the hermaphrodite or androgyne appears as an ideal in various philosophical and poetic texts; the hero who plays the woman's role, modeled on the figure of Hercules with Omphale, reappears as an epic topos in Sidney and Spenser; the heroic woman is variously represented, sometimes (like Bradamant or Britomart) in male disguise, sometimes (like Jonson's queens) overtly female, but in the military personae that declared their mastery of the male role as well. Indeed, as these examples suggest, in a Jacobean context the most striking aspect of Mary Frith was probably not her successful manipulation of the gender codes, but her ability to manipulate them from within her lower-middle-class status.

I turn now to some actual cases. Mary Frith is generally treated as unique, and indeed, that is how she presented herself in her public appearances and in what purports to be her autobiography, published two years after her death. It has become clear, however, that female transvestism was a fairly widespread practice, especially among lower-class women, as opportunities for work in the seventeenth century were increasingly limited to men. Research has uncovered a significant number of documented cases of women who served as men, in the army and in other traditionally male occupations, and in some cases even took wives.[5] As a stratagem for upper- and middle-class women, however, the transvestite model might appear to be an exclusively literary one; the likes of Rosalind, Viola, and Imogen surely exist only in the world of drama and romance. But in fact there are at least two well-known cases in the period of women emulating such heroines, successfully disguising themselves as men to escape the restrictions of court or patriarchy.

In 1605, Elizabeth Southwell, one of Queen Anne's maids of honor, eloped with her lover Sir Robert Dudley. The elopement was doubly scandalous since Dudley had a wife living and a family, and had recently converted to Roman Catholicism. Dudley considered himself a victim of the patriarchal system. He was the illegitimate son of the Earl of Leicester; after Leicester's death he presented evidence that his parents had in fact been secretly, though legally, married, and that he was therefore properly the heir to Leicester's estate and title. In this claim he was probably correct: there were witnesses to the marriage still living, and he was able to show that Leicester had offered his mother £700 to repudiate the marriage, which she had refused. Both the earl and his mother subsequently remarried, and neither marriage was challenged. The evidence was probably sufficient, but the courts declined to invalidate the two later marriages and thereby retroactively to bastardize the earl's heirs, and the whole suit was stayed when, on behalf of Leicester's widow and family, Dudley and his supporters were charged in the Star Chamber with criminal conspiracy.

Frustrated and indignant, Dudley left England, as it turned out for good. His companion was both his cousin and his mistress; the couple escaped to the Continent with Elizabeth disguised as Dudley's page – we might compare Lorenzo's flight with Jessica from Shylock's house, or the traveling lovers of Donne's *Elegy* 16. They then lived openly in Lyons, and, despite the bigamy, received a papal dispensation to marry; they subsequently settled in Florence, and Dudley was rewarded by being made Duke of Northumberland and Earl of Warwick in the Holy Roman Empire. These were Leicester's titles; Dudley had found in Roman Catholicism the legitimation of his birth, and he served as a prize catch in the Papacy's attempt to create an alternative, Catholic aristocracy for Protestant England. Though his estates in England were impounded by the crown and sold (thereby beggaring his abandoned wife and daughters: the patriarchy was no friend to unprotected women and children), he was lucratively employed as a military and naval engineer by the dukes of Tuscany. He built himself a splendid palace in Florence – Lord Herbert of Cherbury describes a visit to him there in his autobiography – and was honored and given a villa by Duke Ferdinand II.[6] Few theatrical disguise plots conclude so happily.

A more tragic case was that of Lady Arbella Stuart, James I's cousin, the daughter of his uncle Charles Stuart, Earl of Lennox, and Lady Margaret Cavendish, the daughter of Bess of Hardwick – a marriage that itself had been arranged in defiance of both Queen Elizabeth's wishes and of English law.[7] Since Arbella was in the line of succession, and had, indeed, been implicated in at least one plot to depose James and put her on the throne, the king had a powerful interest in her marriage plans. Throughout her life, numerous candidates had been proposed by her and her family and rejected, first by Elizabeth and then by James. In 1610, ignoring the king's injunction, she secretly married William Seymour, to whom she had been engaged in 1603. When the marriage was revealed, the King's Council committed Seymour to the Tower and placed Arbella under house arrest, initially in Lambeth. When it was found that this arrangement enabled her to communicate easily with her husband, she was ordered to be sent to Durham; but on the journey her health seemed to be affected, and she was allowed to stay in Barnet for some weeks. When the move to Durham once again seemed imminent, she took action. As one biographer describes it, she

pretended to her chaplain's wife, Mrs Adams, that she was stealing out to pay a last visit to her husband, but would be returning in the morning. Mrs Adams helped her to disguise herself by pulling a pair of French hose over her petticoats, putting her feet into russet boots with red tops, and donning a doublet, black hat and black cloak. She wore a man's wig with long locks that partly concealed her face and a rapier at her side.[8]

In this disguise, she fled from house imprisonment, successfully deceiving an innkeeper and an ostler as to her sex, to join the husband with whom James I had forbidden her to live. Seymour managed to escape from the Tower, also in disguise; the couple planned to flee to France. Arbella reached the coast, and actually managed to board a French vessel sailing for Calais, but Seymour missed their rendezvous, and Arbella was arrested at sea and brought back, to be imprisoned in the Tower for the remaining four years of her life.

No doubt the Lady Arbella saw herself as a romantic heroine; but it is hardly hyperbole to say that the literary models offered her the only possible hope of release from the intolerable situation her paternity had placed her in. It is to the point that both these cases involve the negotiation by the women themselves of forbidden marriages: the reversal of gender usurps the patriarchal prerogatives, and represents a radical refusal to be commodified in the marriage market.

Transvestism here is not a romantic fiction but a real antipatriarchal strategy. The question is not how generally feasible such a strategy may have been – obviously there were very few such cases – but how threatening the model they offered – of the woman who appropriated the prerogatives of men – was felt to be. To begin with, we have seen that neither Elizabethan nor Jacobean society finds the most visible symbol of female masculinity, the transvestite woman, sufficiently threatening to enact any law enjoining her behavior. The more basic conventions flouted by Elizabeth Southwell's and Arbella Stuart's behavior, their infractions of the marriage bond and the family system, were certainly covered by statute, though the statutes up to the seventeenth century seem, if we are looking for evidence of patriarchal panic, surprisingly vague.

A striking example is offered by the legislation regarding Dudley and Southwell's primary offence against the sacred unity of marriage, bigamy. Bigamy was a crime under canon law, but the punishment was merely that the bigamous marriage was declared void. It only became a felony in 1604 – the year before Dudley and Southwell eloped. The change in the law had less to do with the sanctity of matrimony than with parliament's attempt to limit and control the authority of the ecclesiastical courts over marriage, and bring it under civil jurisdiction. A particular issue here was the marriage license system, whereby one could purchase a license to marry from the ecclesiastical court, thus avoiding the public scrutiny attendant on the publication of banns: this meant in effect that for a payment to the church authorities, one could marry secretly.[9] There were a number of cases in the sixteenth century of bigamous marriages that had been effected in this way, and were considered valid. The most famous was that of Henry VIII's sister Mary to Charles Brandon, Duke of Suffolk, who had two wives living at the time he married her. The bigamy statute, significantly, coincides with the promulgation of the ecclesiastical canons of 1604, which raised the age of consent from twelve to twenty-one, thereby greatly increasing paternal authority over marriages. What this means is that two years earlier, Southwell and Dudley would not necessarily have had to flee the country to marry. Judicious payments to the right prelates might have done the job.

Anxieties about bigamy unquestionably have patriarchal roots, but in this case they are not, for once, anxieties about the power of women. The bigamist is almost invariably a man. Of women who violated the marriage bond, for example, by adultery, the law took little notice, both before and after 1604: adultery was a spiritual matter, which remained in the jurisdiction of the ecclesiastical courts, and was not prosecutable under the common law. Under canon law it constituted, at most, grounds upon which a husband could repudiate his wife and obtain a legal separation; it was not grounds for what in modern terms would be called divorce; the parties were not free to remarry, and the husband remained liable for the wife's support. The law here did not favor the man: there was no particular advantage to the husband in this situation, and the statutes provided no relief for that universal figure of fun, the cuckold. Indeed, the children of a legally married woman by an adulterous liaison, even if they were disavowed by her husband, were considered legitimate and took the husband's name – Leontes in his attempt to bastardize Perdita would have found no support in an English court.

The laws relating to marriage, then, were not on the whole concerned with infractions. Instead, the law helped both to define the place of women and to keep them in it by guaranteeing but also limiting their property rights, regulating their rights to contract alliances, and on a lower level, by providing the ducking stool for scolds. There were, of course, extralegal measures, such as the charivari and the skimmington, that were adopted to bring social pressure to bear on marriages that appeared aberrant, generally, again, because of a perceived reversal of the gender roles – most often a too assertive wife. Such proceedings were local, occasional and unsystematic; despite the extensive literature addressing the problem of harridans, shrews, and the like, except in the rare cases where the "unfeminine" woman could be defined as a witch, English Renaissance culture on the whole tolerates her.

Perhaps, however, it does more than that: perhaps there is a sense in which it positively wants her around. Within the cultural norms, as Karen Newman observes, "in the daily life of the household, village, and town, women . . . though always ideologically subject, often had authority over men – over their servants and children, over the less wealthy or wellborn."[10] We have seen how the image of Queen Elizabeth in full armor, as a later account put it "like some Amazonian empress,"[11] rallying her troops at Tilbury when the attack of the Armada was imminent, served as a potent argument against Caroline effeminacy, and indicates the degree to which the masculine woman could serve as an ideal. What is less easy to recognize is that it also indicates the changing nature of the ideological discourse of gender roles in the period: the armor is a Jacobean invention; the contemporary account says only that Elizabeth was on horseback and carried a truncheon.[12] The claim that she was in military dress was initially devised as an argument against the pacifist tendencies of King James. The earliest depiction of her in armor at Tilbury is the Caroline engraving in plate 14, a document in the politics of nostalgia. Elizabeth's ubiquitously cited speech to her troops on the occasion is also a later confection; it survives in a variety of versions, but the earliest dates from shortly after the event and was intended for publication. It is a characteristic performance, consciously playing against traditional gender roles. "I know I have the body of a weak and feeble woman, but I have the heart and stomach of a king . . . Rather than any dishonour shall grow by me, I myself will take up arms, I myself will be your general, judge, and rewarder of every one of your virtues in the field."[13] This is not the rhetoric of an Amazon; Amazons do not present themselves as weak and feeble women. It combines the discourse Othello employs when he calls Desdemona his fair warrior with the Petrarchan, and more specifically Spenserian, ideology in which masculine heroism consists of service to a noble lady, and its rewards are not the spoils of war but the favor she dispenses. Indeed, the contemporary account of the event might be called proto-Spenserian: "her presence and princely encouragement, Bellona-like, infused a second spirit of love, loyalty, and resolution into every souldier . . . ravished with their Soveraygnes sight."[14]

General, judge, patron, war-goddess, love object and ravishing image: these are the roles played by this queen, this weak and feeble woman. The paradox is an essential part of the idealization.[15] The elements of masculine clothing that constitute *haute couture* in the period – including weapons, stilettos and poniards – partake of the same ideology: "O my fair warrior!" Women dress not only for themselves and to impress other women, but also to be attractive to men. If masculine attire on women had really been found generally repellent, it would not have been stylish, and we must conclude that there were Renaissance men who (like many modern men) enjoyed finding themselves in the women they admired. Transvestism is for us male to female. For the Renaissance it was – normatively, so to speak – female to male, and it took forms that ranged from the personal style exemplified by Paulina in *The Winter's Tale*, whom Leontes accuses of being "a mankind (i.e. mannish) witch," to those fashionable accessories of which King James complained to the Bishop of London, and on to outright gender crossing, where the transvestism is intended to deceive, and in a number of cases – the number grows significantly larger as the seventeenth century progresses – apparently succeeded in doing so for long periods.

Linda Woodbridge has anatomized the developing disapproval of masculine fashion for women, culminating in two pamphlets published in 1620, *Hic Mulier*, an attack on women in male dress, and *Haec-Vir*, a reply attacking male effeminacy.[16] What is difficult to determine, however, is whether it was the fashion that was new, or only the anxiety it provoked. That the anxiety has to do with how much more sexually exciting the new fashion renders women is clear from the costume as it is described. It is also clear that the excitement is intimately related to the crossing of gender boundaries. The costume, as illustrated on the title page of *Hic Mulier* (plate 16), consists of a "ruffianly (i.e. whorish) broad-brimmed hat and wanton feather . . . the loose, lascivious civil embracement of a French doublet, being all unbuttoned to entice (i.e. to reveal naked breasts) . . . most ruffianly short hair," and a sword.[17] Such women, the anonymous author argues, "have laid by the bashfulnesse of [their] natures, to gather the impudence of Harlots."[18] Woodbridge wonders "whether a doublet and broad-brimmed hat would be enough to make a woman look masculine, if her breasts were exposed,"[19] but this misses the point: what is construed as "masculine" here is precisely the aggressive sexual display, the flaunting of desire. Masculine dress is conceived as empowering and liberating; it frees its wearers, however, not to be like men – to be soldiers, merchants, artisans, heads of households – but to be sexually active women, harlots. Indeed, the association of cross-dressing with prostitution was commonplace; it comes almost

Plate 16 *Hic Mulier*, 1620, detail of title page.

as an afterthought in Lady Politic Would-be's string of hostile
epithets, "A lewd harlot, a base fricatrice, / A female devil, in a male
outside."[20] The idea that being a harlot constitutes masculine
behavior is no doubt paradoxical, but it shows precisely how much
anxieties about women's sexuality, in this or any other period, are a
projection of male sexual fantasies – being masculine in this case
means having constant and promiscuous sex: this is what it is to "act"
like a man; but the deeper implication is that sexual desire, and the
authority to satisfy it, are male prerogatives.

It is easy to understand why from the Jacobean royal perspective
such behavior in women would have seemed genuinely subversive,
undermining both the structure of society and the norms of its
microcosm in the family. As we have seen, however, contexts are
everything: what was high style at court became subversive on the
streets of London, and even this depended on where the critic stood
to make the judgment. The proprieties of gender have everything to

do with the proprieties of social class. Plate 17 is an erotic painting by Isaac Oliver. It shows, on the right, a courtly scene of hunting, music and lovemaking, with active women, passive men, and a now recognizably significant iconography of female fashionable dress. The picture is moralized through the presence of three women on the left in sober dresses; Roy Strong identifies them, from their costume, as "a lady not of the court but of the city, attended by two servants,"[21] who witness the scene but do nothing to inhibit it. The moral is a function of class distinctions, and remains in the eye of the beholder. To the moralizing eye, an impressive variety of social, and even political, evils could be laid at the door of female lust. Mary Queen of Scots' political behavior was made explicable to the English by declaring her a whore. *Malleus Maleficarum*, the classic Renaissance study of witchcraft, observes that "all witchcraft comes from carnal lust, which in women is insatiable."[22] Licentiousness – and, it follows, witchcraft – are, then, of the essence in women. It is significant that Leontes' invective against Paulina, the charge that she is "a mankind witch," is evoked by her attempt to make him accept what he believes to be the child of his wife's adultery.

But what happens if we look at the matter from other social perspectives? The royal viewpoint, as both James's and Leontes' exasperated frustration make clear, was in fact not widely shared. Paulina the "mankind witch" is, after all, a figure of power and virtue, her shrewish tongue is the agent of restoration and reconciliation. Leontes declares her witchcraft, at the play's end, "lawful as eating." How much of an explanation, in short, is patriarchy? To what extent can the concept be said to account for the operation of English Renaissance society at all, to say nothing of English Renaissance theatre companies, their drama, and the fashions and behavior of the women in their audiences?

In Chapter 4, I called attention to the work of several economic and social historians who have shown that, far from being limited to the

Plate 17 Isaac Oliver, *Allegorical Scene: Virtue Confronting Vice*, c. 1590–95.

private and domestic roles that standard modern history allocates to
them, women in Renaissance England constituted a significant part
of the skilled labor force, and in various parts of the country until
well into the seventeenth century enjoyed full rights within a guild
system that modern historians incorrectly but regularly represent as
exclusively male. Women were engaged in practically every craft and
trade, not as surrogates, wives or widows, but as fully responsible
guild members. And yet the patriarchal ideology of the culture is an
undeniable fact. How can we account for the masons' and
carpenters' "systeren and brethren," the women blacksmiths of
Chester, the half of Southampton apprentices who were women,
within a patriarchal structure?

The question, it will be observed, presupposes two totalizing
concepts, patriarchy and women, and as such it can only produce a
totalizing answer. But once again contexts are everything: what was
true for working-class women cannot be generalized to merchants'
wives, nor are the latter measures of the lives of court ladies. The
Renaissance construction of women emanates from a variety of
contradictory discourses. This does not distinguish it from the
modern construction of women (or, for that matter, men), which is
hardly single or unconflicted; but even within its own terms there is
nothing anomalous about it.

Contradictions may be of the essence of a system; and if they are,
then to undertake to resolve them will misrepresent the system. This
is surely the case with that various and conflicted set of ideologies we
call Renaissance patriarchy. It is always in place, descending from
God himself, but despite the fact that it claims to represent the
natural order of the world, it is also always threatened – this is an
essential element in the way any patriarchy conceives itself. The
contradictions between ideology and behavior form much of the
dynamic of patriarchal discourse in the period. Authority exists only
when it is exerted, and it must be exerted over someone – it must,
that is, constantly create or identify its subjects. Its discourse is of

necessity public, and most Renaissance public discourse is in some way implicated in it. Comedies about the management of shrews and tragedies about daughters who disobey their fathers and make disastrous marriages are obviously implicated in it. Those who see in *Romeo and Juliet* and *Othello* attacks on patriarchy misunderstand the nature, and more specifically the representation, of the ideology of the age.

It is an ideology that contains its contradictions by allowing them to be contradictions; the contradictions – what it sees as threatening it – are essential to it, what make it work. It sees itself as always in danger, and exerts its power by always discovering repetitions of a primary fall from grace, which, since this is a patriarchy, was a rebellion against the father. This served as a universal explanation: "He that will forget God," said Queen Elizabeth accounting for Essex's rebellion against her, "will also forget his benefactors."[23] This does not mean that the system was not in fact threatened, or that the threats could invariably be contained – Elizabethan political history is a history of continual and enforced compromise, and the success of the Puritan revolution is a testimony to the ultimate insufficiency of the crown's strategies of containment. It is important to remember that the subjects in this culture, the potential rebels, are manifold: not only women, or children, or the working class. The ideology of male supremacy itself is rigidly stratified, not only horizontally through the class system, but vertically through primogeniture.[24] Younger sons in this system have no entitlements; they must find their fortunes in the professions, or overseas, or through the agency of women in marriage; and patriarchy itself, as we have seen, was neither single nor unconflicted: the patriarchy of fathers impinged on that of husbands, both were at odds with the patriarchy of the crown, and even the crown could be charged with usurping the prerogatives of God the Father. In short, everyone in this culture was in some respects a woman, feminized in relation to someone.

Clearly the culture has an investment in certain attitudes toward women: that they are naturally inferior, subservient, domestic creatures; that they are properly the objects of desire, not in control or independent of it; more abstractly, that they are a medium of exchange. These are ideological assumptions, incorporated in a variety of official discourses throughout the culture, from the judicial to the gynecological, and they have been for the most part accepted by modern history as representing the truth – a single truth – about women's lives. But such an account cannot be sufficient to define the dynamics of gender in the period. Ideology is the least certain of guides to actual behavior.

In short, the ideology of a culture does not describe its operation, only the ideals and assumptions, often refracted and unacknowledged, of its ruling elite. Patriarchy is not a system but, in Karen Newman's words, "a dominant trope through which social relations were perceived, a strategy whereby power was embodied and institutionalized."[25] To define Renaissance culture simply as a patriarchy, whatever the term is taken to imply, is then to limit one's view to the view the dominant culture took of itself; to assert that within it women were domestic creatures and a medium of exchange is to take Renaissance ideology at its word, and thereby to elide and suppress the large number of women who operated outside the family system, and the explicit social and legal structures that enabled them, in this patriarchy, to do so.[26]

In this respect, even the most powerful feminist analyses are often in collusion with precisely the patriarchal assumptions they undertake to displace. Gayle Rubin's brilliant, classic essay "The Traffic in Women" seems to me to fall into this trap, treating the material of structuralist history as if it were neutral data, and not implicated in the ideological assumptions of the discipline itself. I mean by this that to view the standard erroneous claim that the guilds were all-male as simple information will produce quite a different analysis from one which views the error as significant, and perceives the claim as part of a larger polemic. Susan Stuard, in an important critique of structuralist history that has been all but ignored, makes this point; but her example of women operating outside the system is witches.[27] This is surely conceding far too much. It is the women blacksmiths of Chester, the guild members' "systeren and brethren," the female apprentices of Southampton, who reveal how far the dominant ideology of the realm was from defining its limits. They also might reveal how much more open the question of gender roles was for the Renaissance than it is for us.

𖤣

7

Visible figures

Perhaps the Early Modern conception of male and female did not in fact preclude women from operating in the public world; perhaps it only meant that when they did, they were thought of as "masculine." Ben Jonson, no admirer of female independence, praises the Countess of Bedford for having "a manly soul,"[1] just as Queen Elizabeth emboldens her troops by finding within her female body the heart and spirit of a king. So when Portia becomes a legal expert in order to rescue Antonio, she does it as a man: perhaps the cultural point of this dramatic strategy is not that it constitutes a romantic paradox, but that, eccentric though it may be, there is no impediment to her devising it – it is, in fact, devised precisely in the terms provided by the culture's ideology. We might relate the overt masculinity of Portia's behavior to the implicit masculinity exemplified in the careers of such commanding Elizabethans as Bess of Hardwick (considered below) and Frances Brandon, Duchess of Suffolk, niece of Henry VIII and mother of Lady Jane Grey, who, at the age of thirty-eight defied all the hierarchical, patriarchal and social imperatives and braved the outrage of her cousin the queen herself by taking as her husband her secretary and Master of Horse Adrian Stokes, who was not only her social inferior but sixteen years her junior – "has the woman so far forgotten herself as to marry a common groom?" asked the offended Elizabeth, placing Stokes even lower on the social scale than he actually was.[2] Like Bess of Hardwick and Frances Brandon, moreover, Portia devises a way of maintaining her independence within her marriage: this is all part of being "masculine," but it is also something that women can be – not, to be sure, unproblematically. That tense and fluid situation, however, is translated by modern history into a rigid and settled one where women were excluded from the public world of business, negotiation and labor, and remained at home, commodities and a medium of exchange.

How are we to understand the lives of women whose careers do not fit the standard conception of Renaissance female behavior? Elizabeth Cary, Lady Falkland, defied her husband and family by converting, and persuading six of her children to convert, to Roman Catholicism, and despite extraordinary social and financial pressure, made a life for herself that declared its radical independence of everything in her upbringing and social position. Lady Anne Clifford steadfastly resisted the efforts of her husband to force her to assign her property to him; she maintained her position despite the concerted efforts of patriarchal authority, including not only Attorney General Bacon, but even the king himself. This was very heavy artillery to level against someone who, under the law, had few legal rights and was almost entirely subject to her husband.[3] But she was in fact supported in her resistance by the legal system, and ultimately vindicated, though after her death: her consent was necessary, and without it even the king was powerless to alienate her property. Her intractability was, needless to say, a source of severe tension throughout the marriage and was responsible for a good deal of the misery of her life – though it is difficult to see that she would have been happier had she been a "good" wife, yielding to the patriarchal imperatives and thereby enabling her profligate gambler husband to dissipate her fortune. We deal with such figures by declaring them exceptional; but what is it exactly that they are exceptions to?

Of the three cases I shall now consider in some detail, one is a transvestite, and the other two exemplify careers for which transvestism is allowed to stand, notably successful women who, in misogynist discourse, are identified as unacceptably masculine, a harlot and a virago. I am discussing them not because I believe they show that we can generalize about women in the period, but precisely because they show the difficulty of doing so: they are cases that indicate both the complexities and contradictions in patriarchal attitudes, and the radical inconsistency of the construction of the feminine. Unlike women apprentices and guild members, these women are not statistics; they are well-known figures, women who were famous − or, depending on one's perspective, notorious − in their own time, and they constitute a different kind of challenge to our notion of the hegemony of patriarchal structures. We have seen that the only patriarchy that was threatened by generations of women guild members is the patriarchy of modern historians, who have consistently denied their existence. How, then, did the Renaissance power structure deal with highly visible figures who appear to us subversive, and who are certainly, in the Renaissance as we have conceived it, anomalous?

I begin with Penelope Rich. Daughter of the first Earl of Essex and sister of the brilliant and disastrous second earl, her father in 1576, the year of his death, proposed her as a suitable wife for Philip Sidney. She was at this time fourteen, Sidney twenty-two. For four years the matter remained unsettled, though the principals are said to have been fond of each other, and Penelope has traditionally been identified, starting in her own lifetime, as the Stella of Sidney's sonnet sequence. In 1580, however, her guardian applied to the queen for permission to contract another match for her (since her father had died when his children were minors, she was technically a ward of the crown). The bridegroom was Robert Lord Rich, who had just succeeded to his father's barony; the marriage was, in material and social terms, a far more advantageous one. Rich was a peer, and wealthy, whereas Sidney's prospects depended entirely on his own efforts. Penelope apparently objected to the match with Lord Rich, but Sidney did not press his claim, which in any case had never been formalized, and Penelope's consent was, in some form, obtained. During the next ten years she and Rich had six children. According to later testimony, the marriage was always unhappy; Rich behaved badly to her, and attempted to appropriate a great deal of her property, which he was prevented from doing only by the power and influence of her brother. Nevertheless, she cared enough about him to return to him in 1600, five years after they had separated, to nurse him through a dangerous illness.

So far the story is the unexceptional one of a woman, or perhaps a couple, making the best of an arranged marriage. But in 1592 the picture changes. A year after the birth of her last child by Rich, she took as her lover the brilliant and popular Charles Blount, Lord Mountjoy, and lived apart from her husband, mostly with her brother the Earl of Essex, at whose house Mountjoy was also welcome. Hilliard's miniature, reproduced in plate 2, shows a very fancy and, to modern eyes, effeminate young man. By Mountjoy she had five children, and both were active participants in the complex political affairs of Essex, whom Mountjoy succeeded, in 1600, as Lord Deputy in Ireland. Although Penelope was implicated in Essex's rebellion, she alone of those named was never charged. After Essex's execution in 1601, her husband finally repudiated her, and when Mountjoy returned from Ireland upon James I's accession in 1603, she lived openly with her lover as the mistress of his household. It was not until 1605 that Rich moved to obtain a divorce on the grounds of adultery. This was what we would call a legal separation; it stipulated that neither party could remarry during the lifetime of the other, and Rich was required to continue supporting her. Penelope had to sue to force him to comply, but the courts supported her claim.

During this entire period Penelope Rich was not only socially acceptable, she was an active and influential figure, welcome at court and in society. Mountjoy, moreover, was a hero. Victorious in Ireland where Essex had ignominiously failed, he was shown signal marks of favor by Elizabeth. When James I ascended the throne, he was made a Privy Councillor and Penelope became a Lady of the Bedchamber. The earldom of Essex had perished with her brother, but James conferred on her the rank of her ancestor the original earl – this meant that by the king's patent she retained the family honors, and thereby took precedence at court over all the baronesses in the kingdom. *The Complete Peerage* argues that these marks of royal favor prove that the liaison must have been kept secret, but all the evidence indicates otherwise. The fact that Penelope and Mountjoy were lovers was well known; it was even given in evidence at Essex's prosecution. At the time James was showering them with honors they were maintaining a large and sociable house together, and in 1597, four years before Penelope and Lord Rich formally separated, the lovers had all but announced the paternity of their first son by naming him Mountjoy. There was nothing secretive about the arrangement.

In 1605, from the point of view of legal history and patriarchal panic, things become interesting. After Lord Rich obtained his divorce, Mountjoy and Penelope determined to marry. This was explicitly forbidden under the terms of the decree, though it was not therefore illegal: parliament, in revising the marriage laws, had specifically refused to declare such remarriage a felony.[4] It is easy to see why the couple wanted to do it, and perhaps understandable that they thought they could, given the ambiguity of the legal situation. What is surprising is that William Laud, Mountjoy's chaplain, should have been sufficiently persuaded of the validity of their case to perform the ceremony. It is not clear what the merits of the case were thought to be, particularly by a cleric, but this was the sort of situation in which ecclesiastical courts had traditionally been easygoing, permitting occasional discreet infractions of what was felt to be an overstrict rule. On the other hand, this was also probably precisely the kind of situation the act against abuses of the marriage license had been designed to cover.

Penelope's marriage to Mountjoy – he was now Earl of Devonshire – was conducted discreetly enough, at home with a few witnesses. But the couple were hardly private persons, and a great deal was at stake. For the project to succeed, for Penelope to be styled Countess of Devonshire and for her and their children to be protected from counterclaims on Mountjoy's estate by those family members who would be his heirs if he were unmarried, the marriage had to be publicly recognized as valid. The royal sanction would, for practical purposes, have legitimated the matter, but James, who had welcomed and honored them as adulterous lovers, was outraged when they became husband and wife. Penelope was banished from the court, and Mountjoy, though he remained a Privy Councillor, was admitted only in his official capacity. In the king's eyes, Penelope was the worse offender of the two; he told Mountjoy that "you have won a fair woman with a black soul." It was she, after all, who was the bigamist – yet as an adulteress she had been one of the stars of his court. Most of all James never forgave Laud, and eleven years later refused a preferment Buckingham had asked for him citing his "flagrant crime" of having performed the marriage ceremony. Laud did an annual penance for the act for the rest of his life.

Mountjoy died of a fever less than four months later. By this time it was clear that the marriage would not be validated, but he had made careful testamentary provision for Penelope and their children, and all Penelope's claims on the estate were, after much bitter litigation, upheld by the courts: the law supported her against Mountjoy's family, as it had supported her in her dispute with her husband. When Penelope died a year and a half after Mountjoy, in 1607, she was buried neither as Lady Rich nor as Countess of Devonshire, but simply as "A Lady Devereux,"[5] an unmarried woman from a noble family.

Adultery and fornication, then, were no bar to preferment in this instance. What was perceived as threatening to the patriarchy, and resulted in social ostracism, was the attempt to move back within its norms, the claim of respectability. Our tendency would be to argue that what was intolerable to Renaissance morality was the violation of the family structure, the bigamy, and especially the effective disinheritance of those who thought of themselves as the legitimate heirs. But there are many far more blatant cases in the period, from Charles Brandon, Duke of Suffolk, and the Princess Mary, to the Earl of Leicester; and as we have seen, had Mountjoy and Rich contracted their marriage only a year earlier, the law might well have supported them. The king's behavior is particularly striking, given his enthusiastic support several years later of the Countess of Essex's notorious divorce and remarriage to James's favorite Robert Carr, despite the flagrant misrepresentations involved, and the necessity for suborning the judges and ultimately for packing the court.[6] In this case the king, with considerable difficulty and over strong and courageous judicial protest, was playing Antonio to Carr's Bassanio, Edward to Carr's Gaveston: it is worth remarking the extent to which, at the center of this patriarchy, the obligations of patronage and homosocial bonding in fact took precedence over the sanctity of marriage.

My second case of a well-known woman with a notably successful career that does not fit the standard view of gender roles is Elizabeth, Countess of Shrewsbury – the famous Bess of Hardwick.[7] She has been largely romanticized by modern biographers; in her own time she was formidable, and on occasion dangerous, even to the interests of the queen herself. Edmund Lodge, in 1791, summed up more than two centuries of hostile criticism when he described her as "a woman of a masculine understanding and conduct; proud, furious, selfish and unfeeling."[8] Doubtless, had her "masculine . . . conduct" been the work of a man, it would have been found admirable, but her story also illustrates the ways in which the patriarchal system could be made to work for and by women. She began with serious disadvantages. She was born in 1527; her father died when all five of his children were minors, putting his small Derbyshire estate into the wardship of the crown, by which it was systematically impoverished.

Bess (I will call her this to distinguish her from Queen Elizabeth, who will also figure in this narrative) was married at the age of fifteen to the thirteen-year-old Robert Barlow. Since she had only a minimal dowry, she was not in any material sense a good match, but the marriage was part of a complex scheme to preserve the Barlow property from precisely the situation the Hardwicks had fallen into, the custody of the Court of Wards – to protect the minor children, and the family as a whole, from the depredations of institutionalized patriarchy. It succeeded in its aim, but it brought Bess little in the way of money or security. Her husband died a year and a half later – there were no children, since the marriage, as was common in such youthful matches, had been unconsummated. Her widow's portion amounted to one-third of Barlow's small estate, perhaps £50.

In 1547, at the age of twenty, she married Sir William Cavendish, a prosperous civil servant twenty-two years older than she, and a widower with three daughters. This radically transformed both her status and her prospects. Cavendish was a courtier valued by Henry VIII; he was the younger brother of George Cavendish, Wolsey's retainer and biographer. As a younger son, he had no inheritance, but he became rich through his abilities, and through a good deal of pragmatic opportunism. He began his career in Wolsey's household, survived his fall and worked for Thomas Cromwell, survived Cromwell's fall and continued to serve the crown. He served it throughout the radically Protestant years of Edward VI, and through those of Mary as well, during which he and Bess found it expedient to become Roman Catholics. They were expert at playing both sides – during Mary's reign both the queen and her half sister Elizabeth stood as godparents to Cavendish children, as, more astonishingly, did the father and sister of Lady Jane Grey. Cavendish was shrewd, practical, and exceptionally able; and though his second wife brought him no property, he found a true soulmate in her. Within a few years she was not only managing their several households, but keeping all the accounts. They acquired a good deal of property, which was held jointly during their lifetimes – meaning that, since the title belonged to whichever spouse survived, their minor heirs (they had eight children) would be protected from the Court of Wards. They found a way to make the system work for them.

A good part of that way consisted in Cavendish's embezzlement of funds from his office in the treasury. In 1557 a discrepancy of over £5,000 was discovered in his books. Skimming the crown revenues was commonplace, and was considered one of the perks of the civil service; and there was probably a political motive behind Mary's wish to remove Cavendish, along with a number of other dubiously Catholic bureaucrats, from positions of authority. Nevertheless Cavendish's action was clearly illegal, and he was unable to account for most of the missing money, which had presumably gone into the building of Chatsworth and the furnishing of his several other establishments. To repay so large a sum would have been ruinous, requiring the liquidation of most of his and Bess's property. While the matter was pending, Cavendish died, leaving Bess a widow with an immense debt to the crown.

What made the debt manageable was the death of Queen Mary in the following year. The Cavendishes had supported Princess Elizabeth when it was unfashionable and even dangerous to do so – this, indeed, may have been one of the things that Mary distrusted in them – and the new queen rewarded Bess by bringing her to court as lady-in-waiting. She quickly found a third husband there, Sir William St. Loe, Captain of Elizabeth's guard and Chief Butler (i.e. chief of protocol). St. Loe was well off, old landed gentry, and he must have known of Bess's precarious financial position. But if one can judge from the few letters that survive from the long periods when he was in London and she in Derbyshire, he adored her. The queen eventually remitted all but £1,000 of the debt; the money was paid by St. Loe. When he died eight years later, in 1565, her own property was unencumbered, and since they had had no children, she was the sole heir to his considerable property, a rich widow with absolute control over her fortune.[9]

So far, Bess had beaten the system by a combination of good luck, good management, and what must have been extraordinary charm. We always assume that what constituted success for women in the Renaissance was marrying well, but it would not be correct to say that on the whole Bess had married well. Her first marriage could scarcely have been in her control; in it she was merely a pawn in a game in which she could hardly even hope to be a player. Her second marriage, to Cavendish, looked like a good match, but ended disastrously, and the only element of luck in her ultimately successful negotiation of her difficulties was the convenient death of Queen Mary. St. Loe was unquestionably a good match for her; the fact that he found her a good match for himself would have been entirely due to her powers of intellect, charm and persuasion – she brought with her a ruinous debt. Nor is it even correct to say that she backed the right horses: she was shrewd enough to back all the horses, and both useful and persuasive enough to make it work. She also, obviously, had very accommodating husbands, though St. Loe's payment of her debt was no more than good business, preventing the depletion of estates it was clearly in his interest to preserve.

At this point Bess could have retired to Chatsworth and lived comfortably on her now large income. That she chose not to do so is an index to her ambition both for herself and her children. Her position as a widow was secure, but the route to social advancement was always through marriage. She was now an exceedingly good match, even for a wealthy man; and she married the wealthiest man at court, the recently widowed George Talbot, Earl of Shrewsbury. This was advantageous for both of them; aside from the money involved, their lands abutted in many places. But for Bess, considerable negotiation was necessary: in Elizabethan marriages where both sides owned property, the land settled on the wife was hers only in her lifetime; it could not be passed on to her children by a previous marriage. Bess was past childbearing, and she and the earl therefore used their children to consolidate their own position. The marriage contract stipulated that two of Bess's children should marry two of the earl's. The extraordinary indenture for this arrangement survives; here is a summary of it:

Gilbert Talbot, the Earl's second son, then aged fourteen . . . was to marry Bess's second daughter Mary, who was twelve. If Mary died before the marriage or "before carnal knowledge between them," then Gilbert was to marry Bess's youngest daughter Elizabeth . . . If Mary was bereft of Gilbert by some disaster, then she was to marry one of the Earl's other sons . . . A further marriage was proposed between Bess's eldest son, then eighteen, and the Earl's youngest daughter, who was at most eight at the time. Again all mischance was covered by offering alternative brothers and sisters in descending and ascending order of ages. In the event, all the partners originally chosen lived and did as they were told.[10]

To begin with, the marriage seems to have been a success; but from 1569 the earl and countess were totally occupied with the care of Mary Queen of Scots, who had been put into their keeping by Elizabeth. That they should have been chosen for this complex and dangerous office indicates the depth of the queen's trust in them, and also the degree to which she was willing to use her most loyal supporters. Bess was equal to the challenge; her husband was not. Over the years – Mary was his prisoner until 1584 – the cost of maintaining her severely depleted his resources, and ultimately caused irreconcilable quarrels between him and his wife. Bess, however, used the situation to her own financial advantage, renegotiating their marriage settlement to substitute property for cash when Shrewsbury was short of money.

Bess also, in a move of astonishing boldness, arranged a marriage between her last daughter and the eighteen-year-old Charles Stuart, the younger brother of the Earl of Darnley, and therefore the uncle of the future James I and brother-in-law of their prisoner Mary Queen of Scots. Stuart, through his mother, the Countess of Lennox, had a claim on the English throne, and Elizabeth therefore had a powerful interest in any marriage he might contract. The matter was accomplished while Stuart was traveling with his mother, and Bess briefly entertained them. The young couple were betrothed and married in the space of three weeks; the match was consummated before word of their intentions could reach London. Elizabeth was understandably furious, and the Countess of Lennox was arrested and imprisoned, but Bess seems to have escaped unscathed.[11] Indeed, if her ambitions were dynastic, she had done much to advance them: her daughter's children would now be in the English line of succession. We have already seen how heavy a price the child of that marriage, the tragic Arbella Stuart, paid for her grandmother's ambition.

Bess survived Mary's attempts to implicate her in treasonable plots; she also survived extended hostilities and lawsuits on the part of her increasingly estranged husband. Though Elizabethan law was, as a whole, certainly biased in favor of men, throughout their long and bitter litigation, and throughout her stepson's subsequent litigation against her after his father's death, the courts consistently supported the countess against the two earls. In her last years she ran a large financial empire, greatly increased her wealth, built two of the most splendid houses in England, founded a dynasty that still survives, and managed her affairs until her death in 1608 at the age of eighty. This is one of the most striking success stories, of either women or men, that the age affords. It is the story of a woman who understood the system, remained within it, and made it work for her. It is not clear how far we can generalize from it, but we should certainly be very wary of dismissing it as an anomalous case. Maybe the only thing anomalous about it is the way our history has recorded it.

My last case history is that of Mary Frith, called Moll Cutpurse, shown in plate 18 as she appears on the title page of Middleton and Dekker's *The Roaring Girl*. I shall consider her as she is presented in contemporary accounts, in the few historical records of her life, and her character in *The Roaring Girl* – the use the transvestite stage made of her. To begin with the ephemeral volume that purports to be her autobiography, it is an extraordinary document, in its way unique. The version of seventeenth-century women's lives recounted in it may well include a large component of fantasy, but there is no other fantasy about the lives of Renaissance women that is anything like it.

The Life and death of Mistress Mary Frith, commonly called Moll Cutpurse was published anonymously in 1662, three years after her death.[12] The text includes an elaborately allusive introduction by another hand, and a certain amount of heavy moralizing that is clearly editorial; the body of the work itself, however, while not quite literate, is racy and good-humored, with a sexual openness that has more in common with Restoration comedy than with the world of her Elizabethan and Jacobean upbringing. If the volume indeed derives from an original by Mary Frith (it may certainly be, at least in part, from her lips if not from her pen), it shows her to have possessed considerable ingenuity, charm and a strikingly original sensibility.

Here, to begin with, is a summary of her career taken from the *Life*. Her early years are recounted by an editor: she was born around 1584,[13] a middle-class child, daughter of a shoemaker in the Barbican district of London. She had a good education, but would not apply herself, and showed her masculine leanings early:

A very tomrig or rumpscuttle she was, and delighted and sported only in boys' play and pastime, not minding or companying with the girls: many a bang and blow this hoiting procured her, but she was not so to be tamed or taken off from her rude inclinations . . . her needle, bodkin and thimble she could not think on quietly, wishing them changed into sword and dagger for a bout at cudgels. (10)

The Roaring Girle.
OR
Moll Cut-Purse.

As it hath lately beene Acted on the Fortune-stage by
the *Prince his Players.*

Written by *T. Middleton* and *T. Dekker.*

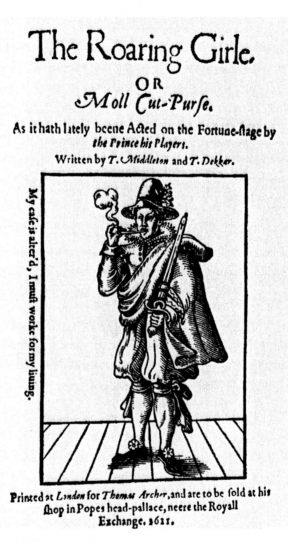

Printed at *London* for *Thomas Archer*, and are to be sold at his
shop in Popes head-pallace, neere the Royall
Exchange. 1611.

Plate 18 Middleton and Dekker, *The Roaring Girl* (London, 1611) title page.

When she grew to be a "lusty and sturdy wench" she was sent into domestic service, but she hated housework. She would not marry, the editor explains, for "above all she had a natural abhorrence to the tending of children" (13) – that "natural" is worth remarking. On the question of her marriage, however, the *Life* is incorrect: she did marry; and her evident suppression of the information is a significant point to which I shall return.

Leaving service, she adopted male dress. Her friends attempted to deal with her eccentricity by hijacking her to Virginia, hoping either that her masculine behavior would constitute a marketable skill in the New World or that the scarcity of women would persuade some colonist to turn her forcibly into a wife, but, in the only episode in the book where she describes herself using traditionally feminine methods, she tearfully persuaded the ship's captain to set her ashore before leaving England. Thereafter she took to a life of petty crime, and soon became notorious as a pickpurse, bully, fortune-teller, receiver and forger. By the 1620s she was, by her own account, the doyenne of the London underworld. She prospered, for the most part as a fence and a pimp; but for all the subversiveness of the career, her impulses were strongly conservative – she was a staunch supporter of Charles I, with no sympathy for the revolution whatever. She describes herself as living in semiretirement during the Commonwealth, with three maids and a small menagerie of nine longhaired dogs, several hunters, a parrot and a monkey. She died in 1659 at the age of seventy-four or seventy-five.

The *Life* is in part a cony-catching pamphlet, a book of comic anecdotes revealing the secrets of cozenage and theft, and proclaiming Frith's own expertise at these arts. Much of its humor arises from episodes in which she deflates male pomposity or takes revenge on male figures of authority who have mistreated her; practical jokes figure largely in it. In these respects the book is unremarkable. It also, however, establishes an area of independence for women – not simply for herself – that is quite remarkable. She claims, for example, to have maintained a universal call service, not only procuring young women for men, but also providing respectable lovers for middle-class wives (she had, she says, no sexual interests of her own). Her striking success at manipulating the patriarchal imperatives is evident in her account of a young wife whom she supplied with a series of well-born admirers. The woman had twelve children, only the first of whom was her husband's. Falling ill and near death, she confessed to her husband the true paternity of their offspring. The cuckold was understandably distressed,

till after her decease . . . coming to condole with him for the loss of my gossip, he roundly taxed me with inveigling his wife into such lewd courses to his no less shame than ruin by such a numerous train of bastards. I bid him be quiet, and if he would follow my advice I would make him a gainer by his hard fortunes, which I effected by procuring him round sums of money from his respective rivals to the maintenance of their illegitimate issue, which they honestly paid; and all was hushed up in a contented secrecy, and he and I as good friends and companions as ever. (72)

The story is characteristic; her criminal success throughout the book derives from her thorough understanding of the system, her ability to work within and through it, to negotiate its double standards, and to do so with complete discretion. For her clients, the appearances are always saved; everyone is represented as satisfied. And though she insists a number of times that at fighting, she is the equal of any man – "I made nothing to crack any man's head with a good baton I had always in my hand . . ., I could use a backsword as well as the best of them" (53) – she often concludes by delivering her adversaries over to the constable, to be jailed or set in the stocks: the law provides her with her ultimate revenge. Indeed, she makes much of her intimacy with officers of the court, powerful lords, the clerk of Newgate, "a nobleman my neighbor" (66), and points with pride to the middle-

MOLL CUT-PURSE.

See here the Presidesse o'th pilfing Trade
Mercuryes second Venus's onely May'd
Doublet and breeches in a Uniform dresse
The female Humurrist a Kickshaw messe
Here no attraction that your fancy greets
But if her FEATURES please not read her FEATS

Pub: by W: Richardson Castle Street Leicester Fields.

Plate 19 Moll Cutpurse: original frontispiece to the *Life and Death of Mrs. Mary Frith* (London, 1662).

class respectability she ultimately achieves for herself: her furnishings, her pets, her three maids, her spotless floors. The figure as the *Life* presents her is represented in plate 19, probably the original frontispiece to the volume, a "female humourist, a kickshaw mess" posed at home, among her possessions. She is an outlaw, but a relatively benign one, capable of violence, but chiefly in self-defense or when sorely provoked, who sums herself up by asserting that "if I had anything of the devil within me, I had of the merry one, not having through all my life done any harm to the life or limb of any person" (64). She sees herself less as a transgressor than as a mediator between the illicit and the licit. In the world she describes, women are fully as active as men, and rather more successful at getting what they want. It is to the point that the enabling figure in this narrative is a transvestite.

In another source, however, Alexander Smith's *History of the Lives of the Most Notorious High-way Men, Foot-Pads, and Other Thieves* (1719), Frith appears as a far more threatening figure, who commits an armed robbery on one of the heroes of the Puritan establishment, her hostility to the Commonwealth expressing itself in violent and material terms:

After Moll had pursued a long and very successful career upon the highway, she robbed General Fairfax, wounded him in the arm, and shot the horses of two of his servants; but she was so closely pursued, that her horse being worn out, she was apprehended, and carried to Newgate. After being condemned, she procured her pardon, by giving her adversary two thousand pounds.[14]

This is one of a number of versions of the episode; elsewhere the amount of the theft is specified as 200 or 250 Jacobuses (roughly £230 and £290 respectively). Fairfax's biographer, John Wilson, says there is "not much evidence for the story,"[15] and there is no version of it in the *Life*, where her thefts of Puritan gold (including a watch filched from Lady Fairfax while at church) are represented as witty and subversive, not violent; but if we are thinking about the anxieties generated by cross-dressing and masculine women, it is not irrelevant that such a story became attached to Mary Frith. And though the robbery was a failure, the narrative nevertheless testifies to a more general success: the £2,000 she is said to have paid to procure her release was an enormous sum in the period, far more than an indemnity for the theft would have warranted. The Moll Cutpurse in this story is very prosperous, or has very prosperous (and generous) patrons.

The documentary evidence for the most part reveals an attractive and popular, if outrageous, figure, a London character. Her ingenuity and self-confidence are evident, for example, in the court record of a 1621 suit against her, under the name "Mary Markham *alias* Frith, *alias* Thrift, *alias* 'Malcutpurse'." Markham was in fact her legal name; as Mark Eccles has shown, she married Lewkner Markham in 1614,[16] a fact that is not mentioned in the *Life*, and one she might well have wished to conceal considering how important a part of the persona both her lack of libido and her independence of men constitute. The marriage was obviously not a success: in 1624 she claimed that "Markham . . . hath not lived with her this tenne years or thereabouts," which would have been the entire period of the marriage. During this period, however, she nevertheless asserted her married status as a way of evading several actions brought against her in which she is described as a spinster – the persona was always manipulable. The 1621 suit charges her with false arrest and imprisonment; an indignant witness calls her "a notorious and infamous person, and such a one as was well known & acquainted with all thieves & cutpurses," and she defends herself by claiming to have a royal warrant to examine thieves for the retrieval of stolen property, asserts that through her efforts "many that had had their purses cut or goods stolen had been helped to their goods again and divers of the offenders taken or discovered," and warns the witness "to go before he was beaten."[17] The warrant was never produced, and is not mentioned again, either in the court record or the *Life*, but both her reliance on intimidation and her claim to be at heart an agent of the crown and an upholder of good order figure prominently in the *Life*.

She was so popular in London, indeed, that presenting her publicly was good business. In 1611 she appeared in a solo performance at the Fortune Theatre, wearing boots, breeches and a sword, singing and accompanying herself on the lute. The performance was certainly not impromptu, since it is announced as forthcoming in

the epilogue to *The Roaring Girl*; a large audience was obviously
expected, and no trouble anticipated from the authorities, and both
she and the theatre management must have made money out of it.
This brief stage career formed part of the charges against her when
in 1612 she was called before the ecclesiastical court to answer
accusations of immorality and immodest behavior, including the
wearing of men's clothes:

and then and there she voluntarily confessed that she had long frequented all
or most of the disorderly and licentious places in this city, as namely she hath
usually in the habit of a man resorted to alehouses, taverns, tobacco shops, and
also to playhouses, there to see plays and prizes [i.e. prizefights]; and namely
being at a play about three-quarters of a year since at the Fortune [Theatre] in
man's apparel, and in her boots, and with a sword by her side, she told the
company there present that she thought many of them were of opinion that
she was a man, but if any of them would come to her lodging they should find
that she is a woman, and some other immodest and lascivious speeches she also
used at that time. And also sat there upon the stage in the public view of all the
people there present, in man's apparel, and played upon her lute and sang a
song.

She confessed in addition to blasphemy, drunkenness, and
consorting with bad company, but

being pressed to declare whether she had not been dishonest of her body and
hath not also drawn other women to lewdness by her persuasions and by carrying herself like a bawd, she absolutely denied that she was chargeable with
either of these imputations.[18]

It is evident that for Mary Frith to dress as a man was in general
inflammatory, in particular sexually, and that her habitual costume
(hardly a disguise) formed a large element in the success of both her
actionable theatrical performance and her continuing fascination for
a variety of male inquisitors, formal and informal. There is a
significantly paradoxical element in the charges brought against her:
her male dress outrages female modesty, but it is her assertion that

she is really a woman, with its implied challenge to the male libido, that is taken to be "immodest and lascivious." Her masculine attire and comportment are, moreover, assumed to constitute licentious behavior that is specifically female, implying that she is a whore and a bawd. As a transvestite she had, in the words of *Hic Mulier*, "gathered the insolence of Harlots" – the feminine here, in a particularly clear way, is constructed out of the masculine. But, in contrast to the claims of the consummate procurer and panderer of the *Life*, the charges relating to female sexuality are the only ones she denies.

For all the moral indignation of the court record, a certain excitement is evident as well: it was clearly impossible not to respond to this figure. Even John Chamberlain's disapproving account of her management of the penance imposed on her by the court on this occasion includes both rueful admiration and a genuine appreciation of her theatrical talents:

This last Sunday Moll Cutpurse, a notorious baggage (that used to go in man's apparel, and challenged the field of divers gallants), was brought to [Paul's Cross], where she wept bitterly and seemed very penitent, but it is since doubted she was maudlin drunk, being discovered to have tippled of three quarts of sack before she came to her penance: she had the daintiest preacher or ghostly father that ever I saw in pulpit, one Ratcliffe of Brazenose in Oxford, a likelier man to have led the revels in some Inn of Court than to be where he was, but the best is he did extreme badly, and so wearied the audience that the best part went away, and the rest tarried rather to hear Moll Cutpurse than him.[19]

Frith's manipulations are clear in this account. She necessarily underwent the penance in female dress, but her habitual usurpations of both gender and class conventions remain uppermost in the observer's mind – Chamberlain tells how she used to wear male clothing, and "challenged the field of divers gallants," dressed as well as any courtiers or dandies. Her tears initially appear to be the badge of her femininity; but they are revealed as having no more to do with her gender than her costume has – they signify not repentance but defiance, and the intolerable deal of sack is yet another challenge to masculinity, a testimony to her ability to drink any man under the table. Chamberlain then proceeds to impugn the manliness of the one man in the scene, "the daintiest preacher" he ever saw, fit only to be a dancing master to young law students wasting their time. If Chamberlain's moral feelings remain outraged, he is in no doubt about the success of the performance.

The Moll Frith of the *Life* gives a particularly defiant version of this incident. While she stood at her public penance, she says, her confederates worked the crowd, cutting garments and stealing purses, and she observes that far from reforming her mode of dress, the punishment only confirmed her detestation of "the finical and modish excesses" of women's apparel – "they might as soon have shamed a black dog as me with any kind of such punishment" (43–5). In fact, however, after this time she seems to have deferred to the moral censors to the extent of adopting an ambiguous garment, a male doublet above and a skirt or petticoat below. She describes herself subsequently wearing full male drag only once, on a dare; this time her appearance precipitated a riot, and though she won her bet, she avows "my great content to see myself thus out of danger, which I would never tempt again in that nature" (46–8).[20] Her androgynous costume, however, unlike male dress, had the advantage of its singularity: her sense of herself in the *Life* is strongly conditioned by assertions of her self-generated and unparalleled nature, which is manifest in her clothing.

Indeed, the most serious challenge to her sense of herself comes not from judicial humiliations or public indignation but from the presence in London of a version of herself, her mirror image,

a contemporary of mine as remarkable as myself, called Aniseed-water Robin, who was clothed very near my antic mode, being an hermaphrodite, a person of both sexes; him I could by no means endure, being the very derision of nature's impotency, whose redundancy in making him man and woman had in effect made him neither . . . being but one step removed from a natural changeling, a kind of mockery (as I was upbraided) of me, who was then counted for an artificial one. And indeed I think nature owed me a spite in sending that thing into the world to mate and match me, that nothing might be without a peer . . . but contrariwise it begot in me a natural abhorrence of him with so strange an antipathy that what by threats and my private instigating of the boys to fall upon and throw dirt at him, I made him quit my walk and habitation that I might have no further scandal among my neighbors, who used to say, "Here comes Moll's husband." (45–6)

"Clothed very near my antic mode": this figure parodies Moll, but also threatens to socialize her in an unendurable way, to "mate and match" her; and just as her husband Markham has been expunged from her narrative, she runs Robin out of town to preserve her uniqueness, which by now is precisely the uniqueness of her costume.[21]

The Moll Frith who appears in the biographical and documentary sources is a wit and trickster, an outlaw, though on the whole not dangerous; and, partly as a function of her outlaw status, glamorous and on occasion even tempting. Middleton and Dekker's version of her in *The Roaring Girl*, in the specifically theatrical context of cross-dressed boy/women and class transgressions, softens and romanticizes her, but it also accurately reflects both the essentially conservative sensibility and the middle-class aspirations of its original. Indeed, the play makes similar claims for the theatre itself; it might be designed as a disarming reply to Rainoldes or Stubbes, demonstrating that beneath the stage's transgressive costume beats a chaste and true heart. Nevertheless, the play's titular epithet was designed as an oxymoron, overstepping a variety of boundaries, starting with those of gender. In standard usage, the roaring was always male, and roaring boys were characteristically upper class or gentry, their riotous behavior an assertion of aristocratic privilege. It was behavior that, though uncivil, was also conceived to be specifically masculine; man's "natural perfection is fierce, hardy, strong in opinion," etc., as Sir Thomas Elyot's taxonomy of gender, cited above, testifies. A working-class "roaring girl" gets everything backwards. Moll's transgressiveness in the play, however, is all in the service of good order and social justice. Her underworld credentials are clearly established – she has a circle of thieves and cutpurses with whom she speaks in canting language – but she serves essentially as an interpreter of their world to the middle-class world of the drama. She is, in fact, the Moll Cutpurse that "Mary Markham *alias* Frith, *alias* Thrift, *alias* 'Malcutpurse'" in 1621 was to represent herself to be, an honorable, comic, sentimental peacemaker, who does not take purses, but recovers them.

The sexual challenge the historical Mary Frith represented has a more complex vitality in the play. Refiguring an episode credited to Long Meg of Westminster,[22] she faces down and humiliates the odious Laxton, gallant and seducer, vowing

> To teach thy base thoughts manners! Thou'rt one of those
> That thinks each woman thy fond flexible whore (3.1.72–3)[23]

and takes on herself not only the defense of womankind, but the overturning of gender roles themselves:

> What durst move you, sir,
> To think me whorish? . . .
> In thee I defy all men, their worst hates
> And their best flatteries, all their golden witchcrafts
> With which they entangle the poor spirits of fools:
> Distressèd needlewomen and trade-fallen wives -
> Fish that must needs bite, or themselves be bitten
> . . . Howe'er
> Thou and the baser world censure my life,
> I'll send 'em word by thee, and write so much
> Upon thy breast, 'cause thou shalt bear't in mind:

Tell them 'twere base to yield where I have conquered.
I scorn to prostitute myself to a man,
I that can prostitute a man to me!   (3.1.88–112)

It is men here who practice witchcraft and seduction; women are
"fish that must needs bite" (the fisherman, presumably, not the
baited hook) to avoid being bitten. The reversal of roles is in fact a
reflection of the play's vision of society, with its profound confusions
of gender. Middleton and Dekker spell out the cultural implications
of Mary Frith's forthcoming indictment for acting like a whore by
dressing like a man.

Laxton has earlier been sexually excited by Moll, not only by her
masculinity, but by her metamorphic quality as well. She appears
wearing a male jerkin over her woman's duster -- since the role was
played by a boy, this was a way of indicating that she is "really" a
woman; the historical Moll at this time was still wearing breeches.
The gallants offer her tobacco (smoking was a male pastime, hence
the ecclesiastical court's charge that Mary Frith frequented tobacco
houses) and, though they know she is a woman, address her as
"sirrah." To Laxton, she "has the spirit of four great parishes, and a
voice that will drown all the city!" – if this sounds like ambivalent
praise, it is not represented as such. When Moll attacks and defeats a
bully carrying a rapier, Laxton swears he will love her forever for
performing "gallantly" and "manfully" (2.1.247–62). Laxton is
captivated by her ability to be everything to everyone, but his praise
also has an obviously autoerotic element:

She slips from one company to another like a fat eel between a Dutchman's
fingers. (2.1.206–7)

He particularly admires Mistress Gallipot's characterization of Moll:
"Some will not stick to say she's a man, and some, both man and
woman" (2.1.209–10). Laxton likes the polymorphous quality of
this; but he clearly admires most of all the double model it provides
for his fantasy life:

That were excellent: she might first cuckold the husband and then make him do as much for the wife! (2.1.211–12)

Moll's male persona implies a universal sexual prowess; but Laxton also takes it as indicating how forthcoming she will be for him.

But Laxton's admiration, of course, constitutes the most dubious of tributes to the woman who plays the man's role. As Marjorie Garber points out, his name implies that he "lacks stones," he is a man without balls.[24] Moll is surrounded by men who are less than men; the play is full of references to impotence, castration, false phalluses, countertenors; it even includes a character named Sir Beauteous Ganymede, whose function in the plot is negligible, but who is, in the semiotic structure of the play, all but essential. If these are the men who admire and fear Moll, what is she to a "real" man, a man who is as fully able and willing to play the man's role as she is?

The only man presented as admirable in the play is Sebastian Wengrave; the main plot concerns his attempt to marry his sweetheart Mary Fitzallard in defiance of his mercenary father's wishes. And in this plot, despite Moll's inflammatory behavior, outrageous costume and underworld connections, she is revealed to be at heart a good bourgeoise. Her function is to facilitate Sebastian's marriage, to defeat the patriarchal menace in favor of the patriarchal virtues. These she also exemplifies: though she is committed to a single life, it is, she assures us, a life of chastity – she is, indeed, with the exception of Mary Fitzallard, the only unquestionably virtuous woman in the play. In a toned-down version of the procurement service described in the *Life*, all the tradesmen's wives flirt and look for lovers among their customers – in this version of the story Moll herself is exculpated. It is no accident that Sebastian's fiancée is also named Mary: the Roaring Girl declares herself, beneath her costume, a model of middle-class feminine behavior. And by the same token, Mary, as part of the ruse to accomplish the marriage, disguises herself as a boy; and Sebastian, in a passage we have already considered, finds that he prefers kissing her as a boy to kissing her as a girl.

In this world, acting like a man is clearly better than acting like a woman, both more attractive and – the point is worth stressing – more likely to lead to an honorable and happy marriage. More than this, it is, in an important sense, a crucial element in acting like a woman. This is the paradoxical lesson that Elizabeth Southwell and Arbella Stuart learned from drama and poetry, those indices to the culture's topoi. And though Moll Frith denies any interest in marriage, the play considers her eminently marriageable, and not merely to the likes of Laxton. Sebastian's father is brought to agree to his son's marriage to the perfectly suitable Mary through a ruse in which Sebastian claims to have transferred his affections to Moll. The ruse is outrageous, but though it has its grotesque aspects, it is not presented as inconceivable or even unlikely, and everyone takes it seriously: Moll is acknowledged to be an attractive and powerful figure, both on stage and off it.[25]

Theatre here holds the mirror up to nature – or more precisely, to culture: this is a world in which masculinity is always in question. In the discourses of patriarchy, gender is the least certain of boundaries. Acting like a man is the most successful, the most compelling way of acting like a woman. *The Roaring Girl* enacts the dangerous possibility that is articulated in innumerable ways throughout this society, from gynecological theory to sartorial style, from the fear of effeminacy to the stage's translation of boys into women and women into boys: that women might be not objects but subjects, not the other but the self.

⋆⋆

Notes

1   Introduction

1 Women were performing in Spain by the 1530s. Most Spanish companies included both women and transvestite boys, and one or the other was prohibited from time to time, but the bans seem to have been relatively ineffective. Female cross-dressing seems to have been considered a more serious moral problem than transvestite boys, and was repeatedly banned (for example in 1600, 1608, 1615 and 1641), which suggests that the ban must have been repeatedly ignored. See Ursula K. Heise, "Transvestism and the Stage Controversy in Spain and England, 1580–1680," *Theatre Journal* 44:3 (October 1992), pp. 357–74. The first actresses appeared on Dutch stages in 1655, to predictably outraged clerical opinion. Holland is not a parallel case because it had had no public theatre before this time, but the event is suggestive and probably points to contrasting Protestant and Catholic attitudes as well. See Simon Schama, *The Embarrassment of Riches* (New York, 1987) p. 408.

2 *Pierce Penniless his Supplication to the Devil*, reprinted in Thomas Nashe, *The Unfortunate Traveller and Other Works*, ed. J. B. Steane (Harmondsworth, 1971), p. 115.

3 Robert Kimbrough, *Shakespeare and the Art of Humankindness* (New Jersey and London, 1990), p. 225.

4 Glynne Wickham, *Early English Stages* 1300–1660 (New York, 1959–81), vol. I, 271–2.

5 Rosemary Woolf, *The English Mystery Plays* (London and New York, 1972), p. 410.

6 A notable exception is T. S. Graves, "Women on the Pre-Restoration

Stage," *Studies in Philology* 22 (1925), pp. 184–97, which cautiously concludes that "the sporadic appearance of women on special occasions may
have been more frequent than has been generally recognized" (p. 196).

7 And attempts to argue it away (as T. S. Graves does in the article cited above)
then take the form of suggesting that the women sponsored or prepared
or paid for the performance, did not act in it.

8 Malone Society, *Collections*, 3 (Oxford, 1954), ed. Jean Robertson and D.
J. Gordon, "Introduction," p. xxii. See also James Stokes, "The Wells
Cordwainers Show: New Evidence Concerning Guild Entertainments in
Somerset," *Comparative Drama* 19 (Winter 1985/6), especially p. 336.

9 Stephen Orgel and Roy Strong, *Inigo Jones: The Theater of the Stuart Court*
(London and Berkeley, 1973), vol. II, 479.

10 Suzanne Gossett, "'Man-Maid, Begone!': Women in Masques," *ELR* 18:1
(1988), p. 109.

11 "She That Plays the King: Henrietta Maria and the Threat of the Actress
in Caroline Culture," in Gordon McMullan and Jonathan Hope, eds., *The
Politics of Tragicomedy* (London and New York, 1992), pp. 189–207.

12 Cited in E. K. Chambers, *The Elizabethan Stage* (Oxford, 1923), vol. I, 371.

13 G. E. Bentley, *The Jacobean and Caroline Stage* (Oxford, 1941–68), vol. I, 25.

14 From William Prynne *Histriomastix* (London, 1633), p. 215: Bentley notes
that Sir Henry Herbert in fact has entries for four performances but one
was canceled "in respect of their ill fortune"; he considers it more likely
that the "hooting and pippin-pelting" took place at the Red Bull, a notoriously rowdy theatre, than at the Blackfriars. See Bentley, *Jacobean and
Caroline Stage*, vol. VI, 226.

15 Chambers, *Elizabethan Stage*, vol. I, 371.

16 Chambers, *Elizabethan Stage*, vol. III, 501: the playbill is reproduced in A.
R. Braunmuller and M. Hattaway, eds., *The Cambridge Companion to
English Renaissance Drama* (Cambridge, 1990), p. 16.

17 Chambers, *Elizabethan Stage*, vol. I, 371.

2 The performance of desire

1 The most significant recent exception, and an excellent discussion of the
issues involved, is Phyllis Rackin's "Androgyny, Mimesis, and the Marriage

of the Boy Heroine on the English Renaissance Stage," *PMLA* 102 (1987), pp. 29–41.

2 The pioneering work on the subject is Jean Howard's, "Cross-Dressing, the Theatre, and Gender Struggle in Early Modern England," *Shakespeare Quarterly* 39:4 (1988), pp. 418–40.

3 See the excellent discussion by Carol Thomas Neely, *Broken Nuptials in Shakespeare's Plays* (New Haven, 1985), especially pp. 105–35.

4 On the idea of the Elizabethan theatre as a literal displacement, see Steven Mullaney, *The Place of the Stage* (Chicago, 1988), *passim*.

5 Malone Society Reprints, 1963, Glenn H. Blayney, ed., lines 208–15. The passage is modernized.

6 The notable Shakespearean exception is Falstaff's disguise as an old woman in *The Merry Wives of Windsor*.

7 The essential discussion of the gender assumptions of modern biology and physiology is Donna Haraway's *Primate Visions* (London and New York, 1989). Coppélia Kahn analyzes the anxieties inherent in Renaissance notions of masculinity in *Man's Estate: Male Identity in Shakespeare* (Berkeley, 1980). On the problematic relation between sex and gender, see especially Valerie Traub, "The (in)significance of lesbian desire in early modern England," in Susan Zimmerman, ed., *Erotic Politics* (London and New York, 1992), pp. 151ff., and Judith Butler, *Gender Trouble* (London and New York, 1990), pp. 6–17.

8 For Jacobean England, the authoritative compendium of anatomical and sexual knowledge was Helkiah Crooke's Μικροκοσμογραφια. *A Description of the Body of Man* (London, 1615), cited below; my summary of the Renaissance physiology of sex is based principally on Crooke, which in turn is a synthesis of standard authorities. I have also been guided by the work of Ian Maclean, *The Renaissance Notion of Woman* (Cambridge, 1983); Audrey Eccles, *Obstetrics and Gynecology in Tudor and Stuart England* (Kent, O. 1982); and Thomas Laqueur, *Making Sex* (Cambridge, Mass, 1990), especially chapters 3 and 4.

9 Such an etiology is not unknown in nature. The sex of alligators is determined by the heat at which the eggs are incubated: if it is 90 °F or over, they are male, if 87 °F or under, they are female. On the question of whether at 88 °F or 89 °F they become androgynes, the authorities are silent.

10 This sounds like a Renaissance ideological fantasy, but it is a view that was firmly maintained by modern biology until 1993, when geneticists finally discovered that there is a gene for femaleness. The New York *Times* reported that

the new work contradicts one of the verities of the sex determination field – that the default mode of a fetus is female, and that it takes the addition of the maleness gene to transform the primal female into a boy. By this notion, the building of a female is a passive business, one that will occur in the absence of any particular signal, while putting together a boy demands the input of the SRY [the gene of masculinity]. (30 August 1994, p. C1)

11 Ambroise Paré, *On Monsters and Marvels*, trans. Janis L. Pallister (Chicago, 1982), pp. 31–2.

12 The French is "je peuz voir," either "I was able to see" or "I could have seen" Garnier. Most English translations (though not the recent version by Donald Frame) take Montaigne to mean the former. For readers of Florio's Elizabethan translation, Montaigne "hapned to meet" Garnier. The travel journal, unpublished until two centuries after Montaigne's death, is included in *The Complete Works of Montaigne*, trans. Donald M. Frame (Stanford, 1948); the story of Marie Germain is on p. 870. Patricia Parker has a superb analysis of the episode and its implications in "Gender Ideology, Gender Change: The Case of Marie Germain," *Critical Inquiry* 19 (Winter 1993), pp. 337–64.

13 Montaigne, *Of the Power of the Imagination*, *Essays*, book 1, 21; in Donald Frame's translation, p. 69.

14 The conflicting classical theories are called *epigenesis*, which holds that sex differentiation is a product of the development of the fetus, and *preformationism*, which views sex as determined at the moment of conception by the nature of the impregnating sperm. For summaries of the ancient controversy, see Michael Boylan, "Galen's Conception Theory," *Journal of the History of Biology* 19:1 (Spring 1986), and Anthony Preus, "Galen's Criticism of Aristotle's Conception Theory," *Journal of the History of Biology* 10:1 (Spring 1977), pp. 65–85.

15 Crooke, Μικροκοσμογραφια, p. 204.

16 Ibid., pp. 216–17.

17 Ibid., p. 271.

18 Ibid., p. 250.

19 Browne, *Christian Morals*, part 1, section 31.

20 *Pseudodoxia Epidemica*, in Geoffrey Keynes, ed., *The Works of Sir Thomas Browne* (London, 1928), vol 1, 246.

21 Ibid., pp. 243–4.

22 Middleton and Dekker, *The Roaring Girl*, Revels Plays edition, ed. Paul Mulholland (Manchester, 1987), 1.2.129–30. See chapter 7, below.

23 Butler, *Gender Trouble*, p. 18.

24 This is not to say that there were no differences between the dress of boys and girls before the breeching, only that the move into manhood for boys was the move from skirts to breeches.

25 Thomas Wright, *The Passions of the Mind in General*, ed. W. W. Newbold (New York, 1986), p. 237.

26 Robert, Burton, *The Anatomy of Melancholy*, 3.2.4.1 (London, 1660; p. 510).

27 Jonas Barish, *The Antitheatrical Prejudice* (Berkeley, 1981), p. 92.

28 Ibid.

29 Laura Levine, *Men in Women's Clothing: Anti-theatricality and Effeminization, 1579 to 1642* (Cambridge, 1994). In what follows I am, in part, summarizing Levine's argument.

30 John Rainoldes, *Th' Overthrow of Stage Playes* ([Middleburg] 1599), p. 11. Here and subsequently the quotations have been modernized. The biblical passage cited is Deut. 23:17–18, rendered in the Authorized Version: "There shall be no whore of the daughters of Israel, nor a sodomite of the sons of Israel. Thou shalt not bring the hire of a whore, or the price of a dog, into the house of the Lord thy God for any vow: for even both these are abomination unto the Lord thy God." The original text concerns temple prostitutes – the words translated "whore" and "sodomite," in Hebrew *k'deshah* and *kadesh*, both derive from the word for "holy"; this is one of a number of prohibitions against the Israelites participating in pagan cults. Translators differed widely over the word the King James scholars render "sodomite," and it was not invariably, or even usually, taken to connote homosexuality. The Geneva Bible reads "There shall be no whore of the daughters of Israel, neither shall there be a whorekeeper of the sons of Israel"; the term in the Vulgate is "scortator," whoremonger or fornicator. As for the dog, *The Interpreters Bible* glosses it "from the context evi-

dently an opprobrious name for a male sacred prostitute" (vol. II, 471). It will be noted that, even in Rainoldes' reading, the passage does not prohibit patronizing whores, whether female or male, it only prohibits Israelites from engaging in the profession – the practice of prostitution is reserved to Gentiles.

31 Rainoldes, Th'Overthrow of Stage Playes, p. 18.

32 William Prynne, Histriomastix (London, 1633), p. 209.

33 Philip Stubbes, Anatomy of Abuses (1585), sig. L8v.

34 Jonathan Goldberg, Sodometries (Stanford, 1992), p. 121. What then is implied by "or worse" – what can be worse than playing the sodomite? If the sodomy here were in fact homosexual, then it would be the sodomized who is worse than the sodomite, the passive partner in the act. Goldberg suggests, unpersuasively, that the distinction is between playing the sodomite and being a sodomite; more helpfully he proposes that "sodomy is a debauched playing that knows no limit . . . or whose limit can only be gestured towards in a supplementary addition." I imagine that, more simply, Stubbes names the worst thing he can imagine, but leaves room for the unimaginable things that are worse.

35 Prynne, Histriomastix, pp. 211–12.

3 The eye of the beholder

1 Peter Stallybrass, "Transvestism and the 'Body Beneath': Speculating on the Boy Actor," in Susan Zimmerman, ed., Erotic Politics (New York and London, 1992), p. 79. The larger theoretical issues are discussed and developed in Peter Stallybrass and Anne Rosalind Jones, Worn Worlds: Clothes and Identity in Early Modern Europe and England, forthcoming.

2 The Countesse of Mountgomeries Urania (London, 1621), p. 60.

3 Thomas Heywood, Apology for Actors (London, 1612), C3v.

4 Ibid., B4r.

5 The letter and translation are in Gāmini Salgādo, Eyewitnesses of Shakespeare (Brighton, 1975), p. 30.

6 TLN 2686–90, corresponding to 5.4.106–10. Modern editors also put Rosalind in a dress at this point, but the costume change is required only by the emendation. The passage, and its editorial implications, are bril-

liantly discussed by Jeffrey Masten, "Textual Deviance: Ganymede's Hand in *As You Like It*," in Marjorie Garber, Rebecca Walkowitz and Paul Franklin, eds., *Field Work: Sites in Literary and Cultural Studies* (London and New York, 1996).

7 Entry for 18 August 1660. *The Diary of Samuel Pepys*, ed. Robert Latham and William Matthews (Berkeley, 1970), vol. I, 224.

8 *Riche his Farewell to the Militarie Profession* (1581), reprinted in Geoffrey Bullough, ed., *Narrative and Dramatic Sources of Shakespeare* (London, 1958), vol. II, 359, 361.

9 Gager in a letter to John Rainoldes, appended to the 1600 edition of *Th'overthrow of Stage-Plays*, p. 55. The documents in the debate between Rainoldes on the one hand and Gager and Alberico Gentili on the other have been collected by Arthur Freeman in *Th'overthrow of Stage-Plays* (New York, 1974). This section of the document, however, is mysteriously omitted from Freeman's collection, but see F. S. Boas, *University Drama in the Tudor Age* (Oxford, 1914) pp. 217−18. J. W. Binns, "Women or Transvestites on the Elizabethan Stage?: an Oxford Controversy," *Sixteenth Century Journal* 5:2 (October 1974), pp. 95−120, provides an excellent guide through the controversy.

10 Rainoldes, *Th'overthrow of Stage-Plays*, p. 97.

11 Stephen Greenblatt, "Fiction and Friction," in Thomas C. Heller et al., eds., *Reconstructing Individualism* (Stanford, 1986), p. 47.

12 Alan Bray, "Homosexuality and Male Friendship in Elizabethan England," in Jonathan Goldberg, ed., *Queering the Renaissance* (Durham, N.C., 1994), pp. 40−61.

13 Katharine Maus, "Horns of Dilemma: Jealousy, Gender and Spectatorship in English Renaissance Drama," *ELH* 54:3 (Fall 1987), pp. 561−2.

14 After the enactment of the canons of 1604, parental consent was required for the marriage of children up to the age of twenty-one.

15 *Works of Thomas Middleton*, ed. A. H. Bullen (Boston, 1886), vol. VIII, 77.

16 Alan Bray, *Homosexuality in Renaissance England* (London, 1982), pp. 54−5.

17 The most detailed analysis of the legal situation is by Bruce Smith, *Homosexual Desire in Shakespeare's England: a Cultural Poetics* (Chicago, 1991), pp. 41−53. For a discussion of the judicial issues relating to sodomy, see below, pp. 58−9.

18 The situation is significantly different on the continent; see, e.g., Guido Ruggiero, *The Boundaries of Eros: Sex Crime and Sexuality in Renaissance Venice* (Oxford, 1985).

19 Bray, *Homosexuality in Renaissance England*, p. 77.

20 Ibid., p. 75.

21 1.1.23.

22 *Othello* 2.1.116. Partridge glosses *work*, "to 'do the deed,' to 'perform,' i.e. to copulate." *Shakespeare's Bawdy* (New York, 1948), p. 223.

23 John Aubrey, *Brief Lives*, ed. Oliver Lawson Dick (Ann Arbor, 1957), p. 11.

24 Paul Seaver, *Wallington's World* (Stanford, 1985), p. 49.

25 Henry Peacham, *Minerva Britanna or a Garden of Heroical Devices* ... (London, 1612), no. 48. The association of sodomy with counterfeiting also appears in the charges against Marlowe.

26 To my knowledge, the only instance of political capital being made of King James's homoeroticism is in the scurrilous *Corona Regia* (1615), almost certainly by the German Catholic satirist Caspar Schoppe (Scoppius), but maliciously credited to James's supporter Isaac Casaubon and published with a false imprint. This makes much of James's conferring on his favorites the title of *Magnus Cubicularius tuus* (Knight of your Bedchamber), praises the king for so successfully mixing lust with religion, and compares him with the notorious Heliogabolus. James, outraged, offered a reward for the identification of the author, which was not claimed until 1639. I am indebted to Winfried Schleiner for this reference.

27 Lucy Hutchinson, *Memoirs of the Life of Colonel Hutchinson* (London, 1906), p. 69.

28 *Letters of King James VI & I*, ed. G. P. V. Akrigg (Berkeley, 1984), p. 431.

29 See Jonathan Goldberg, *Sodometries* (Stanford, 1992), pp. 70ff.

30 January, lines 56–7.

31 Gloss on line 59.

32 See Goldberg's discussion of the poem and the relationship it implies in *Sodometries*, pp. 63–81.

33 See Eve Kosofsky Sedgwick, *Between Men* (New York, 1985), pp. 1–48.

34 Valuable readings of the play along this line are Simon Shepard's *Marlowe and the Politics of Elizabethan Theatre* (New York, 1986), pp. 198ff., and

Goldberg's *Sodometries*, pp. 105ff.; Emily Bartels gives a shrewd critique of the argument in her chapter on the play in *Spectacles of Strangeness* (Philadelphia, 1993).

35 Smith, *Homosexual Desire in Shakespeare's England*, p. 220.

36 David H. Thurn, "Sovereignty, Disorder, and Fetishism in Marlowe's *Edward II*," *Renaissance Drama* NS 21 (Evanston, 1990), p. 136; Gregory Bredbeck, *Sodomy and Interpretation* (Ithaca, 1991), p. 76. Emily Bartels' interesting discussion of the issues surrounding sodomy in the play cites the Holinshed passage, but studiously leaves the method of the stage murder vague (*Spectacles of Strangeness*, pp. 143ff.). David Archer's summary, part of another excellent reading of the play, is strictly correct in remarking that "it is not clear from the text that the spit was used on Marlowe's stage, but its presence betokens the chronicle tradition in which Edward was impaled in a tacit, but grossly parodic, specification of sodomy"; but notice how much more important what doesn't happen to Edward is made here than what does. *Sovereignty and Intelligence* (Stanford, 1993), p. 86.

37 Buckingham graciously remitted the fine. The incident is discussed in Roger Lockyer, *Buckingham* (London, 1981), pp. 101–3.

38 Greenblatt, "Fiction and Friction," p. 51.

39 Dympna Callaghan argues that Malvolio's presentation as the necessary solution to the play's gender crises is in fact more central than it appears: "'And all is semblable a woman's part': body politics and *Twelfth Night*," *Textual Practice* 7:3 (Winter 1993), pp. 428–52.

40 See also Valerie Traub's fascinating discussion of Viola and Olivia as a homoerotic couple; in *Desire and Anxiety* (London and New York, 1992), pp. 130–2.

4 Call me Ganymede

1 "Whoso list to hunt . . .," line 13.

2 *Antony and Cleopatra*, 1.5.17–18.

3 General Prologue, line 691.

4 2.5.5–6.

5 Though mutilation was generally prohibited by the civil law, castration was

permitted by ecclesiastical law under certain circumstances; and the operation in the service of sacred music was explicitly condoned by a papal bull of Sixtus V in 1589. See John Rosselli, "The Castrati as a Professional Group and a Social Phenomenon, 1550–1850," *Acta Musicologica* 60:2 (October 1988), p. 146. Rosselli, indeed, argues that the practice was not considered especially drastic in the sixteenth and seventeenth centuries, and "a castrato could be thought of as an enforced celibate with an unusual chance of securing for his family an income, perhaps a fortune" (p. 150).

6 Booth's citation is from Martial, *Epigrams* 11.22.9–10: "*divisit natura marem: pars una puellis, / una viris genita est*"; *Shakespeare's Sonnets* (New Haven, 1977), p. 165.

7 McLeod's discussion of the sonnet appears in his essay "Imagination," forthcoming. For a brilliant discussion of the breadth of homoerotic possibility in *Twelfth Night* and elsewhere in Shakespeare, specifically addressing the issue of lesbian desire in the plays, see Valerie Traub, *Desire and Anxiety* (London and New York, 1992), especially chapters 4 and 5.

8 Indeed, at the end of Beaumont and Fletcher's *Philaster*, Euphrasia, dressed as the page Bellario, decides to remain permanently in drag and continue serving his lord and lady as both "a Hylas" and "an Adonis," in other words, equally attractive to men and women (ed. D. J. Ashe [Lincoln, Neb., 1974], 5.5.195–204; 2.4.17). For the page Veramour's determination to end *The Honest Man's Fortune* in female drag, see below, pp. 60–1.

9 It should be added that the precedents were often contradictory, and judicial procedure did not invariably follow Coke's interpretations – Castlehaven was convicted of sodomy despite the fact that the sodomy was consensual; the judge based his charge to the jury on an earlier precedent than that cited by Coke.

10 The preamble to a statute of Elizabeth's first parliament (1559) reinstating a statute of Henry VIII against sodomy that had been repealed under Mary I; see Bruce Smith *Homosexual Desire in Shakespeare's England* (Chicago, 1991), p. 47.

11 Smith writes, "the conviction rate for sodomy is significantly lower than the rate for other categories of crime. Between 1553 and 1602 indictments for bestiality in the Home Counties assizes outnumber indictments for sodomy six to one. Once indicted for bestiality, a person was three times

likelier to be convicted and executed than a person indicted for sodomy." Smith, *Homosexual Desire*, p. 49. The ratios tend to obscure the statistical insignificance of these figures: the total number of indictments for sodomy in the half century studied by Smith was six; in Kent during the same period, "they amount . . . to just two indictments out of some three thousand on record – about 0.07 percent" (p. 48). Bruce Boehrer, citing these figures, observes that the bestiality figures are similarly nugatory. "Against this minute quantity, the ten cases of bestiality listed in the same volume may seem a lot, but they still comprise only 0.3 percent of the overall records." "Bestial Buggery in *A Midsummer Night's Dream*," in David Lee Miller et al., eds., *The Production of English Renaissance Culture* (Ithaca, N.Y., 1994), p. 148.

12 Smith, *Homosexual Desire*, p. 51.

13 The basic general study is Foucault's *History of Sexuality*. John J. Winkler's *The Constraints of Desire* (New York and London, 1990) and David Halperin's *One Hundred Years of Homosexuality* (London and New York, 1990) elucidate the classical situation. On Renaissance homoeroticism, the pioneering work of Alan Bray and Eve Kosofsky Sedgwick and the more extended discussions of Gregory Bredbeck, Bruce Smith and Jonathan Goldberg have been cited in previous chapters.

14 3.3; *The Works of Beaumont and Fletcher*, ed. Alexander Dyce (Boston, 1854), vol. I, 542.

15 5.3; ibid., p. 556.

16 Robert Jordan and Harold Love, eds., *The Works of Thomas Southerne* (Oxford, 1988), vol. II, 244–5 (5.4.93ff.).

17 Ibid., p. 191 (2.1.84).

18 Sir John Vanbrugh, *The Relapse*, ed. Curt A. Zimansky (Lincoln, Neb., 1970), 1.3.181–208.

19 *Rochester's Poems on Several Occasions*, ed. James Thorpe (Princeton, 1950), p. 34. ("Well-look'd Link-Boy" means "good-looking torchbearer.")

20 David Riggs, *Ben Jonson* (Cambridge, Mass., 1989), p. 53.

21 The case is discussed in H. N. Hillebrand, *The Child Actors: a Chapter in Elizabethan Stage History*, University of Illinois Studies in Language and Literature 11: 1–2 (Urbana, 1926), pp. 160–3. For a discussion of the writs of impressment, see C. W. Wallace, *The Children of the Chapel at Blackfriars*,

1597–1603, Studies of the University of Nebraska 8:2–3 (Lincoln, 1908), pp. 61–72.

22 Sue-Ellen Case, *Feminism and Theatre* (London, 1988), p. 22.

23 There are none in Chambers, but Theophilus Bird and Hugh Clark are in G. E. Bentley, *The Jacobean and Caroline Stage* (Oxford, 1941–68), vol. II, 377–9 and 406–7. King's examples are cited in "The Versatility of Shakespeare's Actors," in W. R. Elton and W. B. Long, eds., *Shakespeare and Dramatic Tradition* (Newark, Del., 1989), p. 145, based on material in the appendix to Bentley's *The Profession of Player in Shakespeare's Time* (Princeton, 1984). It has been suggested to me that Chapman's dedicatory poem to Nathaniel Field's *A Woman Is a Weather-cock*, beginning "To many formes, as well as many waies, / Thy Active Muse, turnes like thy Acted woman," alludes to Field's excellence in performing female roles; but the reference seems more likely to be simply to the woman of the play's title.

24 This has been repeatedly questioned by modern commentators who find it difficult to imagine roles like Juliet's Nurse or Paulina played by youths. There is certainly nothing inherently inconceivable about the idea of adult men taking elderly or "heavy" female roles, but there is also nothing in the way of evidence suggesting that they did so. Here again, the problem may be only our failure to historicize our notions of verisimilitude; acting old need be no less conventionalized than acting female. Jonson's epitaph on Salomon Pavy (*Epigrams* 120) may perhaps help to quiet some doubts.

25 Both cited by Bentley, *The Profession of Player*, pp. 114–15.

26 And if acting like a woman means acting like the women in the audience, then Tamasaburo and Ganjiro, the masters of the art of female impersonation on the Kabuki stage, do not act or look like women at all, only like something that has for several hundred years been accepted as a representation of women.

27 Eve Kosofsky Sedgwick, *Between Men* (New York, 1985), p. 34.

28 Gloss on lines 56–7.

29 K. D. M. Snell, *Annals of the Labouring Poor* (Cambridge, 1985), p. 270. The pioneering work in the field is that of Alice Clark, *The Working Life of Women in the Seventeenth Century* (London, 1919), the impact of which on historians has been minimal considering the importance of its implications. On the importance of women in the workforce, see also Martha C.

Howell, *Women, Production, and Patriarchy in Late Medieval Cities* (Chicago, 1986), and Margaret L. King, *Women of the Renaissance* (Chicago, 1991), pp. 64ff.

30 Here, as everywhere, we should be wary of generalizing from such data about the lives of Elizabethan women; the figures varied widely from place to place. David Harris Sacks's statistics for the Bristol guilds in the same period show very few women, though their percentage actually increased from the 1530s to the 1630s, from 3.57 to 4.14, and their number more than doubled, from 52 to 118. But Sacks's statistics accord more closely with the usual assumptions about women's place in the workforce: the Bristol female apprentices were employed exclusively in needle trades or household work. What is most important to bear in mind is the existence of such regional differences, the extent to which local options were a part of the system.

31 See Snell's discussion, pp. 270–6.

32 See *The Fourth Part of the Institutes* (London, 1644), p. 5: women are classed here with males under the age of twenty-one and those who own no land – children, servants and laborers. The conference was that of the Australasian Historians of Medieval and Early Modern Europe at the University of Tasmania, Hobart, in February 1994; Crawford's paper, "Gender and Politics in Seventeenth-Century England," is based on research done in collaboration with Sara Mendelson, and forms part of their forthcoming book on the social history of women in England, 1550–1720.

33 "Cross-Dressing, the Theatre, and Gender Struggle in Early Modern England," *Shakespeare Quarterly* 39 (1988), p. 440.

34 I refer to Tennenhouse's essay "The Counterfeit Order of *The Merchant of Venice*," in Murray M. Schwartz and Coppélia Kahn, ed., *Representing Shakespeare* (Baltimore, 1980), and later incorporated in his book *Power on Display* (New York and London, 1986), especially pp. 58–61; to Jardine's "Cultural Confusion and Shakespeare's Learned Heroines," *Shakespeare Quarterly* 38.1 (1987), especially pp. 13–18; and to Newman's "Portia's Ring" in the same issue of *Shakespeare Quarterly*, pp. 19–33.

35 Tennenhouse, *Power on Display*, p. 59.

36 Lisa Jardine, *Still Harping on Daughters* (Brighton, 1983), p. 31.

37 Book I, chapter 12; ed. Albert Feuillerat (Cambridge, 1912), pp. 74ff.

38 Book II, chapter 4, pp. 169–70.

39 Nathaniel Lee, *The Rival Queens* (1677), Epilogue.

40 "Transvestism and the 'body beneath'," in Susan Zimmerman, ed., *Erotic Politics* (London and New York, 1992), p. 68.

5 Masculine apparel

1 Alexander Ross, *Mystagogus Poeticus, or the Muses Interpreter* (London, 1648), pp. 169–70.

2 *Letters of John Chamberlain*, ed. Norman E. McClure (Philadelphiay, 1939), vol. II, 286–7.

3 Ibid., p. 294.

4 See Graham Reynolds' discussion of the painting in *Costume of the Western World: Fashions of the Renaissance*, ed. James Laver (New York, 1951), p. 146: "The lace of the ruff and cuffs and round the yoke of her bodice is dyed with saffron."

5 Barnabe Riche, "Riche his Farewell," in J. P. Collier, ed., *Eight Novels Employed by English Dramatic Poets of the Reign of Queen Elizabeth* (London, 1846), p. 8.

6 *King Henry IV Part One*, 1.3.33–6.

7 Julius S. Held, *Rembrandt Studies* (Princeton, 1991), p. 31.

8 For a discussion of these examples of royal cross-dressing, see my essay *Gendering the Crown*, in Margreta de Grazia et al., eds., *Subject and Object in Renaissance Culture* (Cambridge, 1996). The most thorough analysis of the iconography is by Raymond Waddington, "The Bisexual Portrait of Francis I," in Jean R. Brink et al., eds., *Playing with Gender* (Urbana, 1991), pp. 99–132.

9 See Susan Frye, "The Myth of Elizabeth I at Tilbury," *Sixteenth Century Journal* 23 (1992), pp. 95–114. See below, p. 117.

10 The letter is reprinted in E. K. Chambers, *William Shakespeare* (Oxford, 1930) vol. II, 343–4.

11 *Letters of Philip Gawdy*, ed. I. H. Jeayes (London, 1906), p. 28. See Marion Trousdale, "*Coriolanus* and the Playgoer in 1609," in Murray Biggs, ed., *The Arts of Performance* (Edinburgh, 1991), pp. 124–34.

12 Not, apparently, the same Thomas Giles who was the Master of Paul's at the time.

13 Albert Feuillerat, *Documents Relating to the Office of the Revels in the Time of Queen Elizabeth* (London, 1908), vol. III, 409. William Ingram discusses the complaint, which, however, he takes to mean that the Queen's Revels is renting out the costumes to playing companies. This is not what Giles says. "The 'Evolution' of the Elizabethan Playing Company," in John H. Astington, ed., *The Development of Shakespeare's Theatre* (New York, 1992), pp. 16–17.

14 *The Countesse of Mountgomeries Urania* (London, 1621), p. 60. Michael Shapiro discusses a more extended passage on the same theme from the manuscript continuation of the romance in "Lady Mary Wroth Describes a 'Boy Actress'," *Medieval and Renaissance Drama in England* 4 (1987), pp. 187–94.

15 *Conversations with Drummond*, lines 360–2, reprinted in *Ben Jonson*, ed. Ian Donaldson (Oxford, 1985), p. 604.

16 *Henslowe's Diary*, ed. R. A. Foakes and R. T. Rickert (Cambridge, 1961), p. 325.

17 See my *The Illusion of Power* (California, 1975), pp. 5–6. For a recent, brilliant discussion of the economics of costume in Renaissance theatre, see Peter Stallybrass, "Worn Worlds: Clothes and Identity on the Renaissance Stage," in Margreta de Grazia et al., eds., *Subject and Object in Renaissance Culture* (Cambridge, 1996).

6   Mankind witches

1 Sir Thomas Elyot, *The Boke named the Governour*, ed. Donald W. Rude (New York, 1992), 1:xxi, p. 93.

2 Karen Newman, *Fashioning Femininity* (Chicago, 1991), p. 16.

3 Only a trope, however: Jonson was strongly misogynistic, and disarms his heroines even as he empowers them. See my essay "Jonson and the Amazons," in Elizabeth D. Harvey and Katharine Eisaman Maus, eds., *Soliciting Interpretation* (Chicago, 1990), pp. 119–39.

4 *Areopagitica*, in Stephen Orgel and Jonathan Goldberg, eds., *John Milton* (Oxford, 1990), p. 267.

5 R. Dekker and L. van de Pol, *The Tradition of Female Transvestism in Early Modern Europe* (London, 1989).

6 Information about Elizabeth Southwell and Sir Robert Dudley is from the *DNB* under "Dudley," P. M. Handover, *Arbella Stuart* (London, 1957), pp. 216–17, and David Durant, *Arbella Stuart* (London, 1978), p. 151.

7 Since Lennox, through his father the Earl of Darnley, had a claim on the English throne, the royal assent was required for any marriage he might contract. For information about Arbella Stuart, in addition to the *DNB* (under "Arabella"), Handover's *Arbella Stuart* (see note 6) and Durant's *Arbella Stuart* (see note 6), see Sara J. Steen, "Fashioning an Acceptable Self: Arbella Stuart," *ELR* 18 (1988), pp. 78–95.

8 Handover, *Arbella Stuart*, p. 275.

9 See Martin Ingram, *Church Courts, Sex and Marriage in England, 1570–1640* (Cambridge, 1990), pp. 19–150 *passim*, and Sir Simonds D'Ewes, *A Compleat Journal . . . both of the House of Lords and House of Commons throughout the Whole Reign of Queen Elizabeth* (London, 1693), pp. 555–61.

10 Newman, *Fashioning Femininity*, p. 18.

11 J. E. Neale, *Queen Elizabeth I* (New York, ND), p. 308.

12 Susan Frye has traced the changing accounts of the incidents in "The Myth of Elizabeth I at Tilbury," *Sixteenth Century Journal* 23 (1992), pp. 95–114.

13 See Jasper Ridley, *Elizabeth I* (London, 1987), p. 286.

14 Cited in John Nichols, *Progresses . . . of Queen Elizabeth* (London, 1823), vol. II, 535.

15 Margaret L. King gives an excellent account of the political androgyny cultivated by Elizabeth and other Renaissance female rulers; see *Women of the Renaissance* (Chicago, 1991), pp. 157ff. For Elizabeth's manipulation of her image, see Susan Frye, *Elizabeth I: the Competition for Representation* (Oxford, 1993), and Roy Strong, *Gloriana: the Portraits of Queen Elizabeth I* (London, 1987).

16 Linda Woodbridge, *Women and the English Renaissance* (Urbana, 1986), pp. 139–51.

17 Sig. A4; quoted in Mary Beth Rose, "Women in Men's Clothing: Apparel and Social Stability in *The Roaring Girl*," *ELR* 14:3 (Autumn 1984), p 373.

18 Quoted in Woodbridge, *Women and the English Renaissance*, p. 145.

19 Ibid.

20 Jonson, *Volpone*, 4.2.55–6.

21 Roy Strong, *The English Renaissance Miniature* (London, 1983), p. 157.

22 Lawrence Stone, *The Family, Sex, and Marriage in England, 1500–1800* (New York, 1979), p. 315.

23 The remark was made to William Lambarde; cited in The Arden Shakespeare edition of *King Richard II*, ed. Peter Ure (London, 1956), p. lix.

24 And even this varied regionally: Heather Dubrow has pointed out to me that the county of Kent still followed the law of gavelkind, i.e., inheritance was divided among the heirs, rather than going to the eldest son. As with the question of women in the guild system, regionalism is as significant an issue in matters of inheritance and status within the family as are gender and class.

25 Newman, *Fashioning Femininity*, p. 18.

26 On the necessity for considering conflicting discourses within patriarchal structures, see Margaret Ezell, *The Patriarch's Wife* (Chapel Hill, 1987), James Turner, *One Flesh* (Oxford, 1987) and Heather Dubrow, *A Happier Eden* (Cornell, 1990).

27 Susan Mosher Stuard, "The Annales School and Feminist History: Opening Dialogue with the American Stepchild," *Signs* 7:1 (Autumn 1981), pp. 135–43.

7 Visible figures

1 Jonson, "On Lucy, Countess of Bedford," *Epigrams* 77.13.

2 The remark, with a portrait by Hans Eworth no longer thought to represent Brandon and Stokes, is included in Roy Strong, *The Elizabethan Image* (London, 1969), p. 24.

3 E.g., Susan Dwyer Amussen writes in her fascinating study of the lives of Norfolk women that "women were particularly likely to worry about property at the time of their marriage because according to English law they ceased to exist as legal individuals when they married" (*An Ordered Society* [New York, 1988], p. 72). The accuracy of the claim is not in question; the issue is what kinds of generalizations can be deduced from it: clearly it was possible to find ways around the problem of legal nonexistence. For the career of Lady Anne Clifford, see Katherine O. Acheson's edition of *The Diary of Anne Clifford, 1616–1619* (New York, 1995).

4 See S. R. Gardiner, *History of England, 1603–1616* (London, 1863), vol. 1, 378, citing 1 Jac. 1, cap. 2.

5 Sylvia Freedman, *Poor Penelope* (Bourne End, Bucks., 1983), p. 195.

6 D. H. Willson gives a detailed account of the king's extraordinary manipulations to force the unwilling judges to grant the divorce. See *King James VI and I* (Oxford, 1967), pp. 339ff.

7 My summary of her life derives primarily from David N. Durant, *Bess of Hardwick* (London, 1977).

8 Edmund Lodge, *Illustrations of British History* . . . (London, 1791), vol. 1, xvii.

9 This involved disinheriting and dispossessing St. Loe's younger brother Edward; but since Edward had attempted to poison William and Bess, the arrangement is not surprising.

10 Durant, *Bess of Hardwick*, pp. 56–7.

11 The *DNB*'s assertion that she too was imprisoned is apparently incorrect; see Durant, p. 87.

12 In the same year a shorter book about her entitled *The Woman's Champion*, obviously based either on *The Life* or on the manuscript from which it derives, also appeared. The only surviving copy of *The Life* in a public collection is owned by the British Library, which reports it lost. My quotations are from the modernized edition by Randall S. Nakayama (New York, 1993), which includes glosses and a facsimile of the original. References to page numbers in this edition are given in the text. Good summaries of the biographical information will be found in the introductions to Andor Gomme's New Mermaid edition of *The Roaring Girl* (London, 1976) and Paul Mulholland's Revels Plays edition of the play (Manchester, 1987), I have also consulted Judith Petterson Clark's annotated facsimile, which includes a comprehensive synthesis of the documentary sources and the widely scattered research (unpublished dissertation, Miami University, 1989).

13 The date given in the *Life* is 1589, but this has been shown to be incorrect; see Gomme's introduction to *The Roaring Girl*, p. xiii.

14 In the 1813 edition of Alexander Smith's *History of the Lives of the Most Notorious High-way Men, Foot-Pads, and Other Thieves*, published under the pseudonym Captain Charles Johnson, p. 386.

15 John Wilson, *Fairfax* (London, 1985), p. 122.

16 Mark Eccles, "Mary Frith, The Roaring Girl," *N&Q* NS 32 (March 1985), p. 66.

17 See Margaret Dowling, "A Note on Moll Cutpurse – 'The Roaring Girl,'" *RES* 10 (1934), pp. 67–71; this and other records and allusions are discussed in Gomme, ed., *The Roaring Girl*, pp. xiii–xvii, and in Mulholland, ed., *The Roaring Girl*, pp. 12–14.

18 From the *Consistory of London Correction Book*, fos. 19–20. See Mulholland, ed., *The Roaring Girl*, pp. 262–3. The quotation is modernized.

19 *The Letters of John Chamberlain*, ed. McClure, (Philadelphia, 1939), vol. 1, 534.

20 Other contemporary comments on her pre-1612 male apparel are cited in the introduction to Nakayama's edition of the *Life*.

21 Aniseed-water Robin, so called from his trade as a pedlar of aniseed water (used as a carminative), was a familiar London figure, not fictitious. An extraordinary mythology grew up around him. Frith's assumption that he was a genuine hermaphrodite was widely shared; Horner in Wycherley's *The Country Wife* is warned that if he declares himself to be impotent he will be as noxious to women as Aniseed-water Robin was, and Charles Cotton's epitaph for him credits him with twice impregnating himself, and giving birth to a boy and a girl. See Randall S. Nakayama, "The Sartorial Hermaphrodite," *ANQ* (forthcoming).

22 A similar incident is alluded to in the *Life*, pp. 87–8.

23 References to *The Roaring Girl* are to Mulholland's Revels Plays edition. I have corrected a misprint at 2.1.212.

24 Marjorie Garber, "The Logic of the Transvestite: *The Roaring Girl*," in D. S. Kastan and P. Stallybrass, eds., *Staging the Renaissance: Essays on Elizabethan and Jacobean Drama* (London and New York, 1991), p. 224.

25 On Moll as a figure who unsettles conventional notions of female desire and the ways of managing it, and on the play as "a landscape of erotic desire and practice whose contours cannot quite be mapped in twentieth-century terms," see the excellent essay by Jean Howard, "Sex and social conflict: The erotics of *The Roaring Girl*," in Susan Zimmerman, ed., *Erotic Politics* (New York, 1992), pp. 170–90.

Index

INDEX